Kennikat Press
National University Publications
Literary Criticism Series

General Editor
John E. Becker
Fairleigh Dickinson University

CHRISTIAN CRITICISM
IN THE TWENTIETH CENTU

Norman Reed Cary

CHRISTIAN CRITICISM IN THE TWENTIETH CENTURY

THEOLOGICAL APPROACHES TO LITERATURE

National University Publications
KENNIKAT PRESS / 1975
Port Washington, N. Y. / London

Manufactured in the United States of America

Published by
Kennikat Press Corp.
Port Washington, N.Y./London

PN
98
.R44
C3

Library of Congress Cataloging in Publication Data

Cary, Norman Reed.
    Christian criticism in the twentieth century.

    (Literary criticism series) (National university
publications)
    Bibliography: p.
    Includes index.
    1. Criticism. 2. Christianity and literature.
I. Title.
PN98.R44C3   801'.95   75-37785
ISBN 0-8046-9104-5

TO CECILE

ACKNOWLEDGMENTS

I would like to thank Nathan Scott and Emerson Marks for their helpful comments and suggestions as I was writing the manuscript. I am also grateful to the editor of *Christianity and Literature* for permission to include revised versions of articles which appeared in that journal and its predecessor, *Newsletter of the Conference on Christianity and Literature,* as parts of chapters three and six of this book.

CONTENTS

*CHRISTIAN CRITICISM
IN THE TWENTIETH CENTURY*

CHAPTER ONE

CRITICAL AND THEOLOGICAL BACKGROUND

During the past several decades a number of critics have appeared, especially in Britain and the United States, who have brought Christian insights to bear on literature more strenuously and more systematically than ever before. This is not to say that anything like a common approach exists among them; there are probably as many variations of critical attitude and methodology as there are critics. But the fact that they all attempt to relate Christianity to literature tempts one to group them together, to see them as forming something like a movement in the direction of "Christian Criticism." The purpose of this study is to classify and explore the theological principles in the light of which these individuals criticize literature.

It may be asked why Christian Criticism is described as a recent phenomenon. Have there not been, through the centuries, critics who have been Christians and who have brought their faith into their criticism? The names of Sir Philip Sidney, Dr. Samuel Johnson, and Samuel Taylor Coleridge come immediately to mind as examples. The difference between these older critics who were Christians and the new Christian Critics is that in the work of the older critics Christianity was largely implicit, and in the new Christian Criticism it is largely explicit. The older critics, up through the time of Coleridge (who was perhaps the last major critic who was able to do this), could more or less assume that both their readers and the writers they were commenting upon were Christians. The *corpus christianum* was still intact, if not in terms of ecclesiastical unity at least in terms of the expectation that men in the civilized world shared what C.S. Lewis has, in our lifetime, called "Mere

Christianity."

This situation, as everyone knows, has altered radically since the early nineteenth century, to the point that the Christian in the latter part of the twentieth century feels himself in essential opposition to the non-Christianity of society at large. Following the general cultural trend, literary critics as a rule have disassociated themselves from belief in Christianity; as a result the modern critic who wants to deal with literature from a Christian standpoint has not found direct precedent in the literary criticism of the past 150 years, which constitutes what is inevitably the critical milieu for him. So he has had self-consciously to introduce Christianity into his criticism. It is ironic that the Christian Critics who have striven to do this have discovered that the very criticism which seemed hostile or unconcerned with Christianity afforded valuable hints for them. Evidently the critics of the past century and a half have not been able to free themselves entirely from the faith residual in the culture; as the modern theologian Paul Tillich puts it: "The scars of the Christian tradition cannot be erased; they are a *character indelebilis.*"[1] It is appropriate, therefore, in this introductory chapter to discuss first what can be seen in literary criticism as "preparatory" to Christian Criticism.

The second part of this chapter will deal with the theological milieu of the Christian Critics. Because of the "opposition" status of Christianity in a world that is hostile or indifferent to it, the Christian Critics have been forced, in a way that surely would have seemed unnecessary to their forbears in the faith, to spell out their positions as Christians. Furthermore, the body of Christianity, despite growing pressures towards ecumenicity, is still extremely fragmented. There are competing traditions among Christians, and competing theologies within the same traditions. Therefore it is necessary for the Christian Critic to draw his lines carefully, distinctly stating what theological position he is speaking from and what doctrines he is employing in his approach to literature. It is noteworthy that there are aspects of modern theology that show some of the same intellectual marks of the age that literary criticism shows. Certain modern theologies, especially the Protestant theology of Paul Tillich, the Roman Catholic Neo-Thomism, and Anglican Incarnational theology, also offer valuable openings to the world of literature.

Critical Antecedents to Christian Criticism

As already noted, the intellectual world has moved steadily away from Christianity, towards an increasing enchantment with scientific knowledge and techniques, and an increasing distrust of the artistic as well as the religious. An early instance of this attitude is found in Thomas Love Peacock's *The Four Ages of Poetry* (1820), which views the poet rendered useless and anachronistic by the advance of science. Reacting against this scientism, Shelley, in *A Defence of Poetry* (1821), anticipates the attitude of most subsequent critics, when he looks not to Christianity but to poetry for a knowledge superior to science, claiming that "poets . . . are not only the authors of language and of music, of the dance, and architecture, and statuary, and painting; they are the institutors of laws, and the founders of civil society, and the inventors of the arts of life, and the teachers who draw into a certain propinquity with the beautiful and the true, that partial apprehension of the agencies of the invisible world which is called religion."[2] This transferring of spiritual, prophetic power from the religionist to the poet is extremely significant; we shall see this line of suggestion taken up again and again by the Christian Critics.

Whereas Shelley definitely set himself against traditional religion, and as a young man even declared himself an atheist, Matthew Arnold's attitude towards religion was not a positive rebellion but rather a regretful sadness that traditional Christianity was no longer viable in an enlightened age that had exploded its dogmas as incredible fairy tales. "The object of religion is conduct," Arnold wrote. In fact, God means goodness; Luther took the word God to mean *"the best that man knows or can know;* and, in this sense, as a matter of fact and history, mankind constantly use the word." Elsewhere, Arnold says that the notion of God is "a consciousness of *the not ourselves which makes for righteousness."* Anything more elaborate than this in the way of metaphysics or dogmatizing or supernaturalism is "Aberglaube," extra-belief that is literary language wrongly assigned scientific status, the status of factuality. Separating out fact from the poetic power to move one to righteousness, Arnold is led to the famous prediction made in "The Study of Poetry":

The future of poetry is immense, because in poetry, where it is worthy of its high destinies, our race, as time goes on, will find an even surer and surer stay. There is not a creed which is not shaken, not an accredited dogma which is not shown to be questionable, not a received tradition which does not threaten to dissolve. Our religion has materialised itself in the fact, in the supposed fact; it has attached its emotion to the fact, and now the fact is failing it. But for poetry the idea is everything; the rest is a world of illusion, of divine illusion. Poetry attaches its emotion to the idea; the idea *is* the fact. The strongest part of our religion today is its unconsious poetry.[3]

The cycle is now complete. Whereas poetry was once valued for inculcating religious and moral truth, now poetry is seen itself as religious and moral truth, there being no separable revelation or authority. This extreme didacticism, and the fusing of religious and poetic truth, will prove to be a hallmark of much literary criticism after Arnold.

Clearly standing in the Arnold tradition, for instance, are the "New Humanists" of the twentieth century, chiefly Irving Babbitt, Paul Elmer More, and Norman Foerster. They took over from Arnold a trust in the classical temper as well as a suspicion of modern romanticism and science. They also, like Arnold, had the expectation that literature would be a serious "criticism of life," providing, it would seem, the wisdom formerly available from religion. But their view of religion was more complex than Arnold's. They favored traditional supernaturalism as an absolute standard to oppose modern, relativistic "naturalism," and they looked with favor on such antihumanitarian doctrines as original sin. In this they harked back to the British critic T.E. Hulme, who in his *Speculations* protested against contemporary "monism" with the idea that there is a "discontinuity" or radical disjunction between the natural and the supernatural, and who also came down hard for original sin as a central fact of human nature forgotten by the romantics. Paradoxically, however, the New Humanists were chary of committing themselves to "revealed religion," preferring to see the humanistic temper in many religious and cultural contexts.[4] This attitude towards religion comes under attack by T.S. Eliot in several of his essays. In "The Humanism of Irving Babbitt" and "Second Thoughts about Humanism"[5] Eliot charges the New Humanists with being parasitical on religious values and at the same time unwilling to be more than naturalistic themselves, though they castigate others for naturalism.

Nonetheless, in being concerned with the ethical implications of literature, the New Humanists helped create a climate of opinion hospitable to the later Christian Critics. Moreover, their Arnoldian attitude to literature was to become, despite his unawareness of the fact, one of Eliot's own two contradictory positions regarding the relationship of religion and morality to literature; and Eliot's work was to be crucial for the emergence of

Christian Criticism.

Quoting Foerster's assertion in *American Criticism* that he looks for guidance to "Greek sculpture, Homer, Sophocles, Plato, Aristotle, Virgil, Horace, Jesus, Paul, Augustine, Francis of Assisi, Buddha, Confucius, Shakespeare, Milton and Goethe," Eliot charges that "for a modern humanist, literature thus becomes itself merely a means of approach to something else . . . but this trick of making literature do the work of philosophy, ethics and theology tends to vitiate one's judgment and sensibility in literature."[6] However, Eliot's own essays reveal, through the years, a moralism and theologism similar to that which he atrributes to Foerster and the other New Humanists. But Eliot's theologism is in tension with just the opposite attitude. Eliot insists that literary criticsm must deal strictly with poetry itself; but he also advocates and practices (more often than not) a kind of criticism that involves moral and theological judgments.

The strictly "literary" criticism has given rise to the New Criticism of the forties and fifties, which generally reflects the insistence of I.A. Richards and Eliot on close reading of the poetic text and the exclusion of biographical and ideological considerations as not properly literary. Eliot's early "Tradition and the Individual Talent" (1917) is a famous manifesto for this approach. "Honest criticism and sensitive appreciation is directed not upon the poet but upon the poetry," he warns; he concludes by reminding the reader that "this essay proposes to halt at the frontier of metaphysics or mysticism, and confine itself to such practical conclusions as can be applied by the responsible person interested in poetry. To divert interest from the poet to the poetry is a laudable aim: for it would conduce to a juster estimation of actual poetry, good and bad." A few years later, in "The Function of Criticism," Eliot states that "a critic must have a very highly developed sense of fact," for the limits of the realm of criticism are narrow: "I do not deny that art may be affirmed to serve ends beyond itself; but art is not required to be aware of these ends, and indeed performs its function, whatever that may be, according to various theories of value, much better by indifference to them. Criticism, on the other hand, must always profess an end in view, which roughly speaking, appears to be the elucidation of works of art and the correction of taste."[7]

Do these strictures preclude a criticism that takes theology into account? Eliot's own work would suggest not. The remarks on criticism in "Tradition and the Individual Talent" rest on the assumption that artistic creativity, rather than being an expression of the artist's personal beliefs, is a process of depersonalization: "feelings, phrases, and images" are stored in the poet's mind, which acts as a medium, a catalyst, by which they are united into new combinations. Nonpoetic beliefs, "emotions," do not enter the process. The "beliefs" embodied in poetry are thus liable to be the commonplaces of the age, not the idiosyncrasies of the poet. In "Shakespeare and the Stoicism of Seneca" Eliot seems to have the same sort of idea in mind when he writes that "the great poet, in writing himself, writes his time." Thus Dante became the spokesman for the thirteenth century, Shakespeare the spokesman for the sixteenth. But this does not insure that Dante believed in Thomism, or that Shakespeare believed "the mixed and muddled scepticism of the Renaissance." For it is not the business of the poet to believe, but to "express the greatest emotional intensity of his time, based on whatever his time happened to think. Poetry is not a substitute for philosophy or religion."[8]

In such a situation, where a stable world-view obtains, neither the poet nor the critic feels called upon to concern himself deliberately with theological as opposed to literary matters. However, there may not be any sharp distinction between what is literary and what is theological in an age of faith. Dr. Johnson, for example, could make Christian judgments in the course of his literary criticism without feeling deliberate or programmatic about them; in an age when Christianity was commonly accepted, no one would be likely to think that they were eccentric or extraneous. In "Johnson as Critic and Poet" (1944), Eliot recognizes, however, that the modern critic, living in a relativistic age, is tempted to ignore the moral value of poetry altogether and attempt to suppress the fact that he, like all readers, is affected by the "ideas" or "views of life" in poetry. On the other hand, Eliot continues, criticism in our unsettled age has tended, in its attempts to relate literature to life, to bring in aesthetics, philosophy, psychology, and sociology. Looked at one way, this is an enrichment of criticism; looked at from another perspective, there is the danger that literary considerations will become less important than the nonliterary ones. But Eliot will neither praise nor disparage this tendency, observing only, "It is simply that the conditions under which literature is judged simply and naturally as literature and not another thing, no longer prevail."[9]

It seems he is admitting that his earlier distinctions between the literary and the nonliterary, while they may be ideally desirable, are not workable in the modern world. Thus it is not surprising to notice that elsewhere he follows the logic of this reasoning and recognizes that criticism for the twentieth-century Christian in a non-Christian society cannot be purely "literary." This recognition is of primary importance, for it is an attempt by the foremost literary critic of our century to legitimize theological criticism. The later Christian Critics often have taken this as their entrée into criticism.

Many of Eliot's later essays reflect this recognition. In the University of Virginia lectures, he is still a bit hesitant. The lectures are predominantly an attack on modern literature for being untraditional and possessing only partial and perverted insights into the human condition, and at their outset Eliot denies that this sort of judgment is legitimate literary criticism: it is only moralism. And at the close of the final lecture he adds: "All that I have been able to do here is to suggest that there are standards of criticism, not ordinarily in use, which we may apply to whatever is offered to us as works of philosophy or of art, which might help to render them safer and more profitable for us." We could infer from these remarks that he realizes how rigidly conservative and superficial the moralism is in these lectures; but a year later, in the essay "Religion and Literature," he issues his famous call for theological criticism:

Literary criticism should be completed by criticism from a definite ethical and theological standpoint. In so far as in any age there is common agreement on ethical and theological matters, so far can literary criticism be substantive. In ages like our own, in which there is no such common agreement, it is the more necessary for Christian readers to scrutinize their reading, especially of works of imagination, with explicit ethical and theological standards. The 'greatness' of literature cannot be determined solely by literary standards; though we must remember that whether it is literature or not can be determined only by literary standards.[10]

Other essays of this period also apply moral and theological judgments to specific writers; it is noteworthy, in the light of "Religion and Literature," that many of these writers are not products of an age of faith. In "Shelley and Keats" Eliot would like to say, with an eye to his "purist" notion of literary criticism, that one's Christianity is essentially irrelevant to one as a reader. But he has, in fact, as a reader found the beliefs of Shelley distasteful to the point of hampering his reading. To solve this problem he advances a principle: "When the doctrine, theory, belief, or 'view of life' presented in a poem is one which the mind of the reader can accept as coherent, mature, and founded on the facts of experience, it interposes no obstacle to the reader's enjoyment, whether it be one that he accept or deny, approve or deprecate."[11] It is because Shelley's poetry does not give evidence of such a "tenable" philosophy that Eliot can dismiss it as immature.

I would say that the theory of "wisdom" which Eliot develops in his much more sophisticated essay "Goethe as the Sage" is a refinement and amplification of the idea of maturity in "Shelley and Keats." With the great European poets we must take a wide view of criticism, though there still must be a distinction made between literary and extraliterary criticism: "Literary criticism is an activity which must constantly define its own boundaries; also, it must constantly be going beyond them: the one invariable rule is, that when the literary critic exceeds his frontiers, he should do so in full consciousness of what he is doing. We cannot get very far with Dante, or Shakespeare, or Goethe, without touching upon theology, and philosophy, and ethics, and politics. . . ." The purpose of the essay, he concludes, is more than literary:

Whether the 'philosophy' or the religious faith of Dante or Shakespeare or Goethe is acceptable to us or not [and, indeed, with Shakespeare, the question of what his beliefs were has never been finally settled] there is the Wisdom that we can all accept. It is precisely for the sake of learning Wisdom that we must take the trouble to frequent these men; it is because they are wise men that we should try, if we find one of them uncongenial, to overcome our aversion or indifference. Of revealed religions, and of philosophical systems, we must believe that one is right and the others wrong. But wisdom is *logos zunos,* the same for all men everywhere.[12]

There are two other ways in which Eliot views the non-Christian poet. Recalling the complaints of the New Humanists against naturalism and materialism, he praises Kipling for preserving an attitude which is at least not naturalistic: "It is not a Christian vision, but it is at least a pagan vision—a contradiction of the materialistic view: it is the insight into a harmony with nature which must be re-established if the truly Christian imagination is to be recovered by Christians." Even higher praise is given to Baudelaire, for he went beyond Kipling in perceiving the supernatural. He indulged in a kind of satanism which is blasphemous but at least is a sign of spiritual awareness in an age when the possibility of damnation is seldom recognized. Baudelaire's satanism is, moreover, evidence of a deep preoccupation with the central problem of good and evil, a preoccupation which is unusual in a scientific age. At the close of the essay, significantly, Eliot indicates that his own concern with sin, especially original sin, grew not only from his orthodox Anglicanism but also from the influence of T.E. Hulme.[13]

The more universalist type of criticism which Eliot often practices is of prime importance to the Christian Critics. It not only has served to authorize Christian Criticism theoretically, as already indicated, but it has also suggested specific strategies to the Christian Critics. The Baudelaire essay is particularly helpful in dealing with a "negative witness" to Christianity. What Eliot in "Goethe as the Sage" calls Wisdom is similar to what some Christian Critics will call, more theologically, natural or general revelation. Furthermore, though many of the Christian Critics will not share Eliot's insistence on a Hulmean supernaturalism, they will interest themselves in what transcends the materialistic.

Another modern critic who has displayed something of the same ambivalent attitude towards "extraliterary" criticism, and who directly influenced (much to his displeasure) the beginnings of Christian Criticism in England, is F.R. Leavis. In insisting on close reading of the poetic text, he follows I.A. Richards and is often associated with the New Criticism. He always claimed that he was not a theoretician but a critical reader of specific poems. About this claim, Eric Bentley comments: "The assumption is that literature means something, that the meaning or content is bound up with the style or form, and may therefore be discovered by the trained sensibility. Literature means letters, humane letters, men's words. The best literature, as we have already been taught, is the best words in the best order. Literary study, Leavis concludes, means a study of the words and their order." Thus Leavis repeatedly bristles at those who seem to be distracted by abstract philosophizing. He objects to the suggestion by René Wellek that he clarify and systematize the assumptions behind his criticism: "Words in poetry invite us, not to 'think about' and judge but to 'feel into' or become—to realize a complex experience that is given in the words."[14]

Eliot's criticism is also censured by Leavis for being too abstractly Christian and insufficiently concerned with the particularities of literature. Reviewing Eliot's *Essays Ancient and Modern*, Leavis is scandalized at the religiousness in "Modern Education and the Classics," complaining that "there is, in fact, something very depressing about the way in which, nowadays, he brings out these orthodox generalities, weightily, as substitutes for particularity of statement, rigour of thought, and various other virtues we have a right to expect of him." With his new orthodoxy Eliot is abandoning validly literary criticism for something else, Leavis writes in a review of *After Strange Gods:* "moral or religious criticism cannot be a substitute for literary criticism; it is only by being a literary critic that Mr. Eliot can apply

his recovered standards to literature."[15] Consequently, his reaction to
Poetry and Personal Responsibility by Brother George Every, an Anglican
who was one of the very first critics to attempt explicitly to apply theological criteria to literature, was predictable.[16] Leavis's review, entitled "Christian Discrimination" (after the title of an earlier book by Every) exemplifies
the caustic and humorless sarcasm for which Leavis is notorious. His charge
is similar to the one he leveled against Eliot's religiousness, though it is
stated more maliciously:

As for Christian Discrimination, it needs to be said that there can be no substitute for the scrupulous and disinterested approach of the literary critic.
If Christian belief and Christian attitudes have really affected the critic's
sensibility, then they will play their due part in his perceptions and judgments, without his summoning his creeds and doctrines to the job of discriminating and pronouncing. If, on the other hand, he does, like Bro.
George Every, make a deliberate and determined set at 'discriminating Chris-
tianly', then the life of the spirit will suffer damage, more or less severe, in
the ways that Bro. George Every's work merely exemplifies with a peculiarly
rich obviousness. It is fair to add . . . that he represents the most active and
formidable of contemporary 'gang-movements'.[17]

Despite the fact that Leavis condemns philosophizing, he (like Eliot) is at
times a quasi-moralist and philosopher. His rejoinder to Eliot's emphasis on
orthodoxy is an appeal to his own standards of criticism: "Mr. Eliot has no
need to talk hesitantly about the 'need for a religious sense'; he adheres to
a religion and can point to his Church and recite its dogmas. Nevertheless,
those of us who find no such approach to tradition and orthodoxy possible
can only cultivate the sense of health they have." His concern for literary
standards and "a sense of health" seems to be his substitute for religious
belief. In mourning the passing of a literary journal *(The Calendar of
Modern Letters)* which, like his own *Scrutiny*, had been concerned with
"standards" and "health," Leavis seems to feel that literary criticism is the
only basis by which man can maintain culture and interpret his existence:
"Literary criticism provides the test for life and concreteness; where it de-
generates, the instruments of thought degenerate too, and thinking, released
from the testing and energizing contact with the full living consciousness, is
debilitated, and betrayed to the academic, the abstract, and the verbal. It is
of little use to discuss values if the sense for value in the concrete—the experience and perception of value—is absent." Vincent Buckley observes that
not only does Leavis regard literature as "the nodal" expression of values:

he goes further and "passes imperceptibly . . . to the position where he acknowledges values only as they are subjected to the test of literature, and to the suggestion, which we can't help taking up from him, that literature offers us a final definition of values."[18]

This sounds suspiciously like Arnold's high view of "Culture" as the salutary force in the modern scientific, postdogmatic age. It is not surprising that Leavis has an extremely high view of Arnold; he even defends the Victorian critic: "Many who deplore Arnold's way with religion will agree that, as the other traditions relax and social forms disintegrate, it becomes correspondingly more important to preserve the literary tradition. When things are as already they were in Arnold's time, they make necessary, whatever else may be necessary too, the kind of work that Arnold undertook for 'Culture'—work that couldn't have been done by a theologian as such."[19] We can conclude, then, that Leavis mediated the moralism of Arnold, as well as a respect for the literary text, to the Christian Critics and to the school of "Christian Discrimination" in particular.

Ironically, the man to whom Leavis specifically directed his scorn as a representative of that school very clearly reflects his influence. Even before the attack in the pages of *Scrutiny*, Every recognized that Leavis regarded the arts as "the storehouse of recorded values," and furthermore that he was quite justified in attempting to keep a minority sensitive and informed, to supply them with the critical tools with which they could discriminate between good and bad literature, with which they could avoid the sentimentalism and escapism that infects much that passes for creative literature— with which, to use Eliot's word, they could develop and exercise taste. Though he does deplore Leavis's denigration of Eliot's later criticism, and points out that Leavis does sometimes "play the amateur theologian or sociologist to the detriment of his concentration upon the strictly literary-critical side of the job," Every contends that the Christian reader of literature needs not only a sound theology but also the critical carefulness characteristic of Leavis's method.[20] And in *Christian Discrimination*, the book which provided Leavis with a label for the Anglo-Catholic criticism in *Theology*, Every asserts that he is writing in order to influence the taste of a critical minority towards conscious awareness of standards and a transcending of cultural provincialism: purposes shared by Leavis. In fact, he explicitly states his debt to F.R. Leavis and his wife in the introduction to the book: "I owe a great deal to those who have sounded a persistent alarm about the absence of standards in education, culture, and politics, in particular to

Dr. and Mrs. Leavis and their friends of the *Scrutiny* group, who have remained sceptical about the relevance of theology to the problem, though they have never denied that the problem is in some sort a religious one."[21]

But how is taste theologically significant? C.S. Lewis, in reacting to Every's article "The Necessity of Scrutiny," holds that it is not. Salvation, he argues, is not dependent in any way on literature or any other aspect of culture. He notes that the ancient Fathers were very suspicious of culture, and that even John Henry Newman declared that literature, after all, was only the voice of the natural, sinful man. At best, Lewis concludes, culture is merely preliminary and recreative. Every responds to Lewis by agreeing with Leavis that the critical task is to "teach us how to read." But he denies the severe distinction which Lewis makes between the natural activities of the human soul and the supernatural realm of the human spirit; inevitably the "recreation" of the soul, the interests and moral attitudes which come to typify a man—his taste, if you will—affect the salvation of his spirit. The Church has recognized this for centuries, he continues, by making the classical liberal education the foundation upon which are built the studies of philosophy and theology. Thus he is led to remark, again invoking Leavis and his group, that "the educational program of *Scrutiny* seems to me to be in large part, albeit unconsciously, a return to the good traditions of the first two subjects, grammar and rhetoric, in the medieval trivium."[22]

Like many other Christian Critics, Every is concerned lest the Christian way of feeling and imagining become unintelligible to the world at large, which has rejected all supernaturalism for a world of practicality and factuality. If the world is completely secularized, he warns, Christian discrimination may be reduced to "exposing muddle and confusion and concealed irrationality, making ready new forms of expression and communication through the spoken rather than the written word, and through music and song when speech is impossible, until the hour of resurrection come." In the meantime we have art that the Christian can view as religious rather than humanist, for it recognizes "the weakness and sinfulness of man and his need of redemption." We also have various sorts of criticism at the present time, all of which are valuable for elucidating literature; but they all must include the discipline of the Leavis school: "There is no reason why the Marxian, the psycho-analyst, and the theologian should not all simultaneously set to work to analyse the concealed economic motives, the neuroses, and the heresies in modern popular literature ... provided only that none of them think that they can do their work without the aid of the trained critic, and that none expect an instant acceptance of their results. We want as many analyses as possible."[23]

Several years later, Every connects the trend toward the secular fact with a more recent countertendency, which to some degree accounts for the conversion of T.S. Eliot and the reaction of the artistically sensitive against secularism. Every discerns a schism between serious thinking and artistic thinking beginning during the industrial revolution, until at the opening of the twentieth century serious thinkers were reluctant to admit any imaginative element into their intellectual constructions. But the free verse of Pound and the early Eliot represented the breakdown of the scientific world picture, which had already been criticized by such men as Nietzsche, Bergson, and later Freud, all of whom held that the intellect did not give an adequate account of the world and demanded that the irrational in man be recognized. In this context poetry, which is able to engage the irrational, became once again a serious activity rather than an aesthetic frivolity. The ability of the imagination to raise profound questions about man and society and God is apparent in the later poetry of Eliot, in which we see his pilgrimage to orthodox Christianity. In his criticism, too, we see a growing sense of tradition and the need for an "organic" society. And in his journal, *The Criterion*, we see an increasing concern with social issues, though with many of the contributors to the journal during the thirties social concern was expressed in Marxist terms. In Leavis we also see the concern for society, but in terms of a critical elite who would understand that man's deepest insights and feelings will be evident not in pronouncements that can be abstracted from the literary text but in the very style and form of the art. Leavis's concern for man's values was evident even in the twenties, and in a sense he paved the way for the preoccupation with ideology that so horrified him during the following decade. But then the intellectuals became disenchanted with Marxism, and following World War II there emerged a new type of criticism, which was not afraid to "define the outlook of a writer in terms that go beyond the limits of literature" but which also was forced, by the complicated and condensed poetry of such men as Dylan Thomas and Charles Williams, to a close attentiveness to the specificities of poetic speech.[24]

Unfortunately, Every's theories are sometimes more seminal than his practical application of them. He is occasionally guilty, in *Christian Discrimination*, of some strange literary preferences. For instance, he praises Crabbe not for his literary ability but for being the last writer who assumed common values in his audience. And he lauds Charlotte M. Yonge as a

"Christian novelist," a choice which elicited a very strong negative reaction from Q.D. Leavis.[25] In *Poetry and Personal Responsibility*, Every includes some penetrating essays on Graham Greene, Joyce, Charles Williams, and others; but he cannot resist the temptation to rank Kathleen Raine and Edith Sitwell with T.S. Eliot as literary explorers of orthodox Christianity.[26]

Another challenge to Lewis's anticultural bias comes from S.L. Bethell, the other major *Theology* critic. He charges Lewis with taking a stance perilously close to Calvinism, pointing out that the Catholic faith has always seen fit to "baptize the natural order into Christ" (distinguishing those elements worth baptizing, of course) rather than consigning it all to the devil. He also, like Every, objects to the distinction by Lewis between soul and spirit, noting that literary criticism, especially since I.A. Richards, has taken psychological insights into account. With such insights in mind, Bethell contends that unconsciously held attitudes, often those characteristic of the writer's milieu or the result of his own unintellectualized assumptions, are more important than the attitudes which are explicitly articulated. These unconscious attitudes are not located in obvious preachments but in the details of style, a fact which, to his credit, F.R. Leavis recognizes in his criticism.[27]

However, Bethell continues, Leavis does not consistently seem to admit, in his own preoccupation with values, that unconscious assumptions are equally important for the critics, for such assumptions are the basis of "the quality of their insight, the degree of their sensitive understanding of human experience." What is so dangerous today, Bethell contends, is the appearance of so-called *pure* critics, who flaunt their impartiality and condemn what they term critical partisanship; but in fact, he points out, they themselves hold unconsciously to nineteenth-century humanism, which has become universally pervasive in academic circles. These critics, argues Bethell, are the ones who are narrowly dogmatic (in the popular sense of the word), for they lack the intellectual humility of the Christian, who must admit that all human judgments are partial and clouded because they originate from fallen man.[28]

The only salvation from narrow personal prejudices open to either the writer or the critic, Bethell maintains, is in the Church, for it provides the only tradition, the only continuity of belief; otherwise there is only the chaos and flux of the unconscious. Therefore, Bethell advances the proposition that "we must have in the Church a body of really able and informed literary critics who are themselves practicing churchmen, not wholly ignorant of theology." Such critics should inaugurate their own periodical to publish new poetry and prose; they should also reassess the literature of the past on the basis of Christian principles to counter what now passes for literary history, which is "the product of a Whig and free-thinking age, dominated by the still recent success of the Romantic Movement." The new perspective would re-establish the seventeenth-century divines (Andrewes, Donne, Taylor, Barrow, South, and Stillingfleet) and reduce the influence of Hobbes. Leavis, in his *Revaluations*, has by this time followed Eliot and reassessed poetry in the light of the raised status of the metaphysical poets; the reassessment on Christian grounds, Bethell proposes, would "perhaps treat more kindly that modest central line of Christian poets and prose writers, who, with the cultural tide against them, clung to the foundations of their faith." Some of these would be Isaac Watts, Edward Young, and Christopher Smart of the eighteenth century, and Captain Marryat and Charlotte M. Yonge of the twentieth century.[29]

Going even further, Bethell advocates that since the Christian tradition stands in opposition to the intellectual and emotional chaos of the world, Christian writers should write only for other Christians until Christian culture (along the lines of Maritain's *True Humanism* and Eliot's *Notes Towards the Definition of Culture*) be re-established. The poetry produced by such writers would probably be classic in temper, ordered and socially responsible, not individualistic. It would also have an element of romance, in the sense of touching on the mysterious and the intangible, for it would be "an exploration of the fringes of human experience which border on the immanent and transcendent life of God." Then, lest his conception of poetry be thought a restriction to the merely devotional, Bethell assures us that he has in mind a poetry "dealing with every aspect of human and divine activity, but always based upon the acknowledged facts and principles of the Catholic faith."[30] The criterion for acceptability, nonetheless, is strictly limited to Catholicism (Anglican and Roman); and this extremely parochial version of a "great tradition" almost seems worthy of Leavis's scorn for the *Theology* critics. But Bethell's call for an orthodox criticism is evidence of a new level of self-consciousness and confidence that a new and valid kind of theological criticism is possible.

In his later consideration of the relationship betweeen orthodoxy and literature, Bethell seems less sanguine about the possibility of literature written by Catholic Christians solely for Catholic Christians; and he broadens, slightly, his view of a Christian criticism. He does deny that there is anything like a work of art in itself: a work of art inevitably is compounded of attitudes to life, experience, and the world. This means that the critic is brought face to face with the problem of belief and value. Now the Christian Critic does not automatically approve the works of fellow Christians; a writer must produce well-written work or it must be dismissed. But the Christian Critic will do more than pass judgment on the writer's ability to write; he will also examine whether Christianity is central or peripheral to the work, whether what appears to the writer as Christian is really something else; in short, he must examine closely "the quality of insight that is really there; for every glimpse of reality is welcome to the Christian; he has inherited the earth and those who are not against him are on his side." With regard to the non-Christian writer, he will look beneath the level of profession to see what is really there, and applaud anything of value.[31]

Although Leavis had a special influence, historically, on the development of Christian Criticism in Great Britain, his attitudes are not untypical of several of the American New Critics. Of the original "Fugitive School," out of whose writing the New Criticism was born in the United States, we shall first examine Allen Tate, whom R.W. Stallman described as the "spokesman of the Southern school of poet-critics." There is an ambivalence in Tate's writing similar to that in the criticism of F.R. Leavis—which is not surprising, since he, like Leavis, was strongly influenced by Eliot. Like Eliot in his early criticism, Tate is very concerned in his early criticism to establish the autonomy of the poem, and to establish careful reading as the valid critical strategy. Thus, for instance, there is his famous announcement that poetry is "neither religion nor social engineering." He reiterates this idea with the claim, in "The Present Function of Criticism," that poetry is autotelic; the poet as poet is committed to the specificities of language and image, not to political or philosophical or religious abstractions.[32]

Nonetheless, Tate moves away from this narrow view of poetry and criticism so that one of the more recent Christian Critics is able to say of Tate, as well as Eliot, that their "inquiries into the nature of man's life in culture have led them often to move from a consideration of aesthetic and literary problems to a consideration of religious and theological problems." For Tate, as for Eliot, the central difficulty for the poet today is the lack of a living tradition; and he often contrasts the ages of orthodox Christian faith to the contemporary chaos. In "What Is a Traditional Society?" he discusses Eliot's *The Waste Land* as exhibiting the aimlessness of modern life; then he catches himself short, finding it necessary to apologize for a preoccupation which, he feels, does not accord with his pronouncements about what the literary critic should engage in. He calls himself not a poet or a literary critic but a moralist, and offers as a defense only a plea to the reader that he "remember that moralists these days are desperate persons, and must in their weaker moments squeeze a moral even out of modern poetry." But his continuing interest in the problem of the poet in a larger cultural context (exemplified in his essays on E.A. Robinson, Hart Crane, and Emily Dickinson) leads him to broader views of the function of criticism. In "A Note on Critical Autotelism" he defends the New Criticism in surprisingly inclusive terms: "There can be no end to the permutations of the critical relation to literature, philosophy, and religion. The New Criticism offers to the lingering eye as many permutations as criticism in the past has offered, and probably more." In the series of brief reflective queries which constitute "Is Literary Criticism Possible?" he ponders the relation of artistic truth to nonartistic, "absolute" truth: "Is literary criticism possible without a criterion of absolute truth? Would a criterion of absolute truth make literary criticism as we know it unnecessary? Can it have a relevant criterion of truth without acknowledging an emergent order of truth in its great subject matter, literature itself?"[33]

The growing preoccupation with the ultimate implications of literature comes most to the fore in "The Man of Letters in the Modern World," which is thoroughly saturated with Christian ideas, and is surely Tate's version of Eliot's "Religion and Literature." Tate analyzes the basic sickness of the modern world as anthropological: its view of men has been debased until the individual has become an automaton. Automatons in the mass are directed by communication, which has for its purpose conditioning and control. The man of letters, on the other hand, is heir to a tradition which sees man differently. The image of man for him is two-sided. The secularists would deny man the capability of radical evil, but the man of letters perceives that man can still be lost; in fact, "there would be no hell for modern man if our men of letters were not calling attention to it." But Tate also sees man to be capable of radical, personalizing love-in-communion: "Perhaps it is not too grandiose a conception to suggest that works of literature, from the short lyric to the long epic, are the recurrent discovery of the human communion as experience, in a definite place and at a definite time."[34]

The anthropology underlying the critical discrimination of man-in-communion from man-in-the-crowd Tate recognizes to be derived from a source other than literature itself. At this point Tate parallels most closely the language of Eliot's "Religion and Literature": the critical responsibility of the man of letters is "what it has always been—the recreation and the application of literary standards, which, in order to be effectively literary, must be more than literary." What are these "more than literary" standards? Going further than Eliot, Tate declares them to be religious, for the essence of true communication, in which the artist is intimately implicated, is communion through love. But love is not a matter of conscious decision; a man "loves his neighbor, as well as the man he has never seen, only through the love of God. 'He that saith that he is in the light, and hateth his brother, is in darkness even until now.'" Tate has here broken new ground. It would have been helpful if he had clarified some of his ideas. Does he mean, for instance, to recall the theory of Tolstoy's "What Is Art?" that its function is to transmit feelings of human brotherhood? It is clear, however, that Tate has moved substantially beyond his earlier notion of poetry as autotelic. The close of the essay at first glance would appear to be a reiteration of Arnold's call for the preservation of "Culture," but Tate appeals to supernatural sanctions and concludes on a definitely Christian note: "It is the duty of the man of letters to supervise the culture of language, to which the rest of culture is subordinate, and to warn us when our language is ceasing to forward the ends proper to man. The end of social man is communion in time through love, which is beyond time."[35]

The criticism of Cleanth Brooks follows a developmental pattern closely similar to that in Tate's work. As with Tate, Brooks's early essays are largely practical criticism, close reading of poetry to show the superiority of the metaphysical style of paradox and indirection over the thinner poetry of abstract ideology. He severely attacks Yvor Winters, for example, because Winters passes moral judgment on "rational" truth that he abstracts from poetry—a practice which in the end treats the poem as a statement of the poet's beliefs rather than a dramatic presentation of the complexities of experience that stands independent of the poet.[36] Like the other New Critics, Brooks is attempting to reestablish the validity of metaphorical truth, which embodies the richness and contrariety of life, in the face of the modern scientistic tendency to see only generalized and rationalized statements as cognitive. But "metaphorical" is another designation for what other writers call "mythic," and here Brooks is right on the verge of moving from strict explication of poetry to the realm of religion and metaphysics, a movement which he disparages in Arnold and the early Richards. In a lecture delivered at the Jewish Theological Seminary in New York City, Brooks acknowledges, though he does not expatiate on, the relationship of poetry to myth. He defends "the great myths" against the charge that they are mere fairy tales, noting that John Crowe Ransom referred to myths as "great radical metaphors" and arguing that, like metaphors in poetry, they "embody unique insights and are inexhaustible, not susceptible to being reduced to paraphrase."[37] The essay "Christianity, Myth, and the Symbolism of Poetry" is more specific about the relation of poetic and religious language. Both involve symbolic language and myth, but they differ, for "literature always involves an *as-if*. "The literary mode is par excellence that in which we learn what it feels like to be in a certain situation. . . . But religion always involves, it seems to me, some kind of commitment, something deeper than any *as-if*."[38]

In lectures given in 1955 at the Conference in Theology for College Faculty, Trinity College, Connecticut, the approach is frankly Christian. I do not know whether Brooks would call his criticism here literary or something else, but the lectures combine theological themes with themes from his literary criticism. They are addressed to Christians as readers of modern literature, but they deal both with writers who profess Christianity and with those who do not. He warns his audience that the Christian is to pay close attention to work by both types of authors. The non-Christians, for their part, are producing "some of the most spiritually nourishing literature of our time." The committed writers, for their part, are to be approached as artists, not purveyors of "overt preachments," for it is only the element of art that separates what they write from the religious tract.[39]

The "problem of Christian literature" is twofold. First, there is the question of a viable myth as a framework for the modern writer, since he lives in a world where all myth is doubted. Brooks recalls Yeats's "Search for a New Myth" and notes that, although Christianity was finally rejected as an "exploded" and impossible option for Yeats, Yeats did take Christianity seriously as part of his universal system and as a valid protest against modern secularism. Brooks also reiterates his long-standing emphasis on the ironic and paradoxical nature of poetry by discussing the necessity for T.S. Eliot to present the Christian myth indirectly: "We cannot see directly and face to face. We must use symbols and analogies. Eliot quite properly refuses to 'overleap' and 'cheat' the 'conditions of man.' Man is not an angelic intelligence, a pure spirit. He is an embodied soul. Yet that body was created by God as was the world itself. God's purpose can be discerned in that world, and his glory can be shown forth through the creatures of that world."[40]

The second problem is anthropological; like Tate, Brooks sees a major task of literature to be resistance of dehumanizing behaviorism and the reduction of the individual to a part of a manipulated mass perfectible by sociological means. He discusses Hemingway, Faulkner, Eliot, and Robert Penn Warren in terms of their attempts at reasserting a more or less classical view of man. Hemingway's man affirms a stoical courage in the face of a meaningless universe; Faulkner, Eliot, and Warren insist on the ambiguity of human character, on the Hulmean emphasis on original sin, which is at least a partial recollection of the Christian doctrine. But Brooks is at pains always to spell out the relationship of the artists' visions to Christianity. Their anthropologies are seen in the light of theologian Paul Tillich's recognition that in modern culture there is "an increasingly powerful protest against the spirit of industrialism," which produces emptiness and meaninglessness.[41]

The emphasis of Hemingway and Faulkner on courage is regarded by Brooks as "significant and perhaps necessary as a first step in moving back toward the Christian witness." However, as we have seen in the lecture on Eliot, Brooks is not trying to make Christians out of all modern poets. The approach of these artists to Christianity is often only proximate: the artist is primarily committed to the complexity of experience, but even this may be salutary, for it will keep the artist from fashionable deceptions and help him recognize the human situations to which Christianity speaks. The Christian is not to come to modern literature, though, merely to be edified; what the Christian may "get out of" his reading is an increased awareness of the world: "If one of the functions of literature is to help us to fix our eyes otherwhere, another important function and perhaps a primary function is to let us see where we actually do fix our eyes—to reveal the predicament in which we gaze idly at nothing except that which is just beyond our noses and merely beneath our feet."[42] Thus Brooks has been able skillfully to join a specifically Christian vision with the broadly humanistic breadth which is found in the New Critics characteristically.

The Theological Milieu of Christian Criticism

The importance of theological milieu for the development of Christian Criticism has been mentioned above. The predominant school among literary critics, as we have seen, was the New Criticism. It would be difficult to prove that the New Critics were directly influenced by modern theology in the "Fugitive" period. Nevertheless, it is at least coincidental that theology in the first half of the century was involved with several of the same problems that engaged the literary critics. Like Hulme, some early twentieth-century theologians assumed: (1) discontinuity between the natural and the supernatural, and (2) original sin as basic to the human make-up. They were reacting against nineteenth-century romanticism, which was monistic and optimistic about man.

Hulme was specifically opposed to Bergson, for whom the basic reality was the dynamic, creative, evolutionary élan vital or life-force, which is striving to overcome the inertia of static matter. This may seem like dualism, but actually, according to the French philosopher, "matter itself is a kind of by-product of the vital impetus. This creative life-force is the God of Bergson's philosophy." In *Speculations* Hulme counters with a forthright dualism: "It is necessary to realize that there is an absolute, and not a relative, difference between humanism (which we can take to be the highest expression of the vital), and the religious spirit. The *divine* is not *life* at its intensest. It contains in a way an almost *anti-vital* element. . . ." Bergson also stresses spontaneous, intuitive apprehension of the ideal life and love towards which the life-force is pressing. Hulme would label this the merest romantic humanism, again holding to a strict dualism which sees religious perfection as absolutely distinct from human sinfulness: "What is important, is what nobody seems to realize—the dogmas like that of Original Sin, which are the closest expression of the categories of the religious attitude. That man is in no sense perfect, but a wretched creature, who can yet apprehend perfection. It is not, then, that I put up with the dogma for the sake of the sentiment, but that I may possibly swallow the sentiment for the sake of the dogma. . . . Certainly no humanist could understand the dogma. They all chatter about matters which are in comparison with this, quite secondary notions—God, Freedom, and Immortality."[43]

Similarly, there were theologians who reacted against the religious optimism and evolutionism which held sway in Europe and the United States before World War I. The two most influential continental theologians of the latter nineteenth century, Albrecht Ritschl and Ernst Troeltsch, were both firmly in the optimistic tradition. For Ritschl theology was primarily a matter of ethical advancement: faith affirms that there are "transcendental spiritual powers" which aid man to "thrust back the otherwise annihilating forces of Nature." In other words, "God is the needed prop of ethical aspiration, the trustee of our moral interests." Troeltsch concentrated on study-ing the history and development of the world's religions *(Religionsgeschichte)* and saw Christianity in the context of a universal Spirit operating in history, "Spirit that has issued from its transcendent origin, that is striving on and up through all kinds of human error and failure, that in uniform and rational development is conquering by degrees the limitations and hindrances insep-arable from bondage to nature, and is gradually rising by the native powers of immanent purpose to its absolute completion." Furthermore, the law of continuity is central to Troeltsch: there is in no sense an "absolute" which can be separated from history, for "all events are woven into the same web and are of the same general pattern, all are explicable by immanent forces, all are such that an exhaustive interpretation of their emergence can be undertaken with good hopes of success."[44]

Ritschl and Troeltsch, and a host of lesser thinkers in the English-speak-ing world, set the tone of idealism and optimism in theology before World War I. After World War I the pessimism and dualism which we have seen to be major motifs in Hulme came to be major themes in European theology as well. Theology in the United States remained optimistic through the 1930s, for American theology has traditionally displayed a "cultural lag," picking up European theology about a generation later; besides, the effects of the war and even the depression were less severe in America—but the change came nevertheless.

The watershed which separated the old from the new theology was the publication in 1919 of a commentary on Saint Paul's Epistle to the Romans by a young rural pastor in Germany, Karl Barth. Barth went entirely against the idealistic-optimistic direction of nineteenth-century theology, and appealed instead to Kierkegaard and to the Protestant Reformers Luther and Calvin. Any notion of human-divine continuity was strenuously and repeatedly denied, for the world of time, in Barth's view, is radically sepa-rated from the eternal, ontologically and morally. "Every concrete and tan-gible thing belongs within the order of time," he wrote. And "everything which emerges in men and which owes its form and expansion to them is always and everywhere, and as such, ungodly and unclean." Any attempt, in fact, to deny the gap between infinity and finitude, or to bridge it from man's side, is not only futile but sinful, for Barth defined sin as "a robbing of God," which reveals itself in our "drunken blurring of the distance which separates us from God; in our forgetfulness of His invisibility; in our invest-ing of men with the form of God and of God with the form of man; and in our devotion to some romantic infinity, some 'No-God' of this world, which we have created for ourselves."[45]

Barth, unlike Hulme, did not stop here. Hulme's "dogmatism" has to do only with discontinuity and original sin; the only way out of the human dilemma seems to be some sort of stoical discipline. With Barth, on the other hand, the discussion about discontinuity and an unromantic view of man are preparatory to the proclamation of the gift of salvation from God to man from the "other side," in Jesus Christ. Still, Barth's early theology did alter the emphasis of theology by recalling the Kierkegaardian view of human nature and focusing attention on man's lostness.[46]

As Karl Barth brought about the collapse of the older theology in Europe, the optimistic feeling which prevailed a generation longer in the United States was similarly challenged by Reinhold Niebuhr, who was much influenced by Barth yet was distinctly American in his approach, which was socially rather than systematically or dogmatically oriented. In several respects the ideas of Niebuhr, like those of Barth, resemble the ideas of Hulme. Both men are critical of the modern trust in science and progress, ·
because it presupposes an overly confident notion of human achievement. Deplorably, wrote Hulme, "all thought since the Renaissance, in spite of its apparent variety, forms one coherent whole. . . . It all rests on the same conception of the nature of man and all exhibits the same inability to recognize the meaning of the dogma of original sin. In this period not only have its philosophy, its literature and its ethics been based upon this new conception of man as fundamentally good, as sufficient, as the measure of things; but a good case can be made out for regarding many of its characteristic economic features as springing entirely from this central abstract conception." Niebuhr quotes this very passage as an introduction to his essay on "The Easy Conscience of Modern Man" in *The Nature and Destiny of Man*. He perceives a deviation from the more realistic Christian anthropology, which, in the myth of the Fall, recognizes a less attractive side to human nature. This is the great weakness of modern "liberal Christianity," with its superficial acquiescence to commercialism and its complacent optimism. His writings in the 1930s and 1940s made for a reevaluation of the older American liberal view of man and society; the more mysterious complexities of human nature were once again noticed, instead of being shunted aside as old-fashioned. At least one of the contemporary Christian Critics, who has explored the range of human possibility in modern literature, acknowledges Niebuhr's direct influence: Nathan A. Scott, Jr. dedicates

his volume of theoretical criticism "to Reinhold Niebuhr: From whom I learned my first lessons in detecting the religious frontiers of contemporary culture—Whose classroom was for me the place of the first Great Awakening."[47]

We have seen how the predominant theological trend of post-World War I Protestant theology, by rejecting the old romantic optimism and by making a sharp distinction between religion and culture, parallels the thrust of the New Criticism. The stress on original sin in both Hulme and Barth was valuable for Christian Critics, for it enabled them to perceive new depths of human personality and thus be better equipped to deal with the complex, haunted, lost, and demonic characters typical of modern literature. But the notion of discontinuity long precluded serious consideration of creative literature by the theologically minded: literature was an expression of sinful man and, like all his other cultural achievements, was found wanting under the judgment of God. Probably the strongest advocate of this position was W.H. Auden, whose poetry (ironically enough) seems to belie his theoretical denial that "Christian" art is possible. Reflecting the idea that the sacred and the secular are completely disjunctive realms, Auden asserts that "to a Christian, unfortunately, both art and science are secular activities, that is to say, small beer." The artistic imagination is purely natural, and is liable to be moved by "certain objects, beings, and events, to a feeling of sacred awe." This smacks of pantheism. To the Christian, on the other hand, the truly sacred is not that which naturally arouses awe in the human imagination, but the Christ, who comes "in the form of a Servant who cannot be recognized by the eye of flesh and blood, but only by the eye of faith."[48]

Behind these seemingly facile remarks lies Auden's deep acquaintance with Kierkegaard's view of the aesthetic as only the first stage, surpassed by both the ethical and the religious; each stage is preparatory to the next but transcended only by a leap of faith—there is no evolution from one to the other. Pantheism and the natural worship of the imagination imply a premoral identification with nature and human emotion. But for any moral development to occur, one must cease to float through life attempting to be morally unengaged. One must pass on to moral effort; and finally, realizing that the ideal demands of ethics cannot be met, one must experience the "new life" of faith in personal confrontation with the Eternal.[49]

It might seem curious that Christian Criticism managed to spring up in a theological soil so hostile to human culture. The truth is that there have been theological currents in the twentieth century more amenable to culture, the most important of which is the "theology of culture" in the writings of Paul Tillich. He does not, like the theologians who follow Thomas Aquinas, deal with culture by calling it a kind of "natural" revelation. Instead, he attempts a correlation between the questions posed by man's existential situation, expressed in his cultural creations, and the answers of the Christian message. Thus the study of all aspects of man's cultural life is validated for the theologian, including the examination of his art: "The analysis of the human situation employs materials made available by man's creative self-interpretation in all realms of culture. Philosophy contributes, but so do poetry, drama, the novel, therapeutic psychology, and sociology. The theologian organizes these materials in relation to the answer given by the Christian message." Such an analysis is appropriate because for Tillich culture itself is religious: it has a dimension of "depth"; it is an expression of the human spirit in terms of "ultimate concern," which is what religion is. There is a close relationship, then, between religion and culture which cannot be broken even if "religion" claims to be hostile to "culture" or vice versa; for "Religion as ultimate concern is the meaning-giving substance of culture, and culture is the totality of forms in which the basic concern of religion expresses itself. In abbreviation: religion is the substance of culture, culture is the form of religion."[50]

Also open to theologizing about art is the movement sometimes called Neo-Thomism. Scholasticism was revived in Italy and France in the nineteenth century, and was especially recommended to the Roman Catholic Church by Pope Leo XIII in the encyclical *Aeterni Patris* (1879). As a movement it began to gain ground after World War I, and "by mid-century it had fully emerged as an intellectual force of the first magnitude." Neo-Thomism made available once more the emphasis on natural revelation and the doctrine of analogy—ideas which have provided major themes for the Christian Critics. One of the primary concerns of the Neo-Thomists has been to reconcile the world of the natural and the world of the supernatural. Thus, for example, Jacques Maritain, who became unquestionably the most prominent of the Neo-Thomists, delineates three degrees of knowledge, each proper in its own sphere but all forming a grand synthesis: scientific knowledge, metaphysical knowledge, and supranational knowledge.[51] Elsewhere he goes beyond the rather skimpy references to art in Saint Thomas to construct a full-fledged Neo-Scholastic philosophy of art. He has thus emerged as the leading Roman Catholic theoretician of art in the twentieth century. Anglicans of Catholic bent have also been influenced by Neo-Thomism. It is no coincidence, perhaps, that *Theology,* the organ of the school of "Christian Discrimination," was a conservative "high church" journal; these critics were, as heirs of the Oxford Movement, more at home in the atmosphere of Roman Catholic thought than with Biblicist Protestantism. The two leading Anglican Thomists, Austin Farrer and E.L. Mascall, have written several books which deal with the relation of the natural to the supernatural, with the doctrine of *analogia entis,* and with the meaning of image (the image of God in Christ, biblical typology and imagery) for theology and for poetry.

Likewise growing out of renewed Catholic intellectual ferment is the recognition that art is sacramental and incarnational. T.S.K. Scott-Craig, writing on "Christianity and Poetry," touches all these themes when he recalls that "because of the analogy between things natural and supernatural, because of the poetic character of reality, Christ was able to bring sacramental worship to His people. More than once during the course of His ministry Christ took ordinary food and drink—bread, wine, fish (basic nourishment of the common folk)—and used them as effective symbols of the Divine Reality which was drawing near in Him, the Kingdom come and to come."[52] Sacramental theology and speculation on natural religion have been perennial emphases in Anglican thought ever since the seventeenth-century Caroline Divines. It was the Tractarian Movement, however, which sparked new interest in these areas.

Anglicanism shares many of these concerns with Roman Catholicism, of course, but what has often been seen to be peculiarly Anglican is the focus on the Incarnation. Archbishop Ramsey is thus able to say that "it is almost a commonplace that a theology of Incarnation prevailed in Anglican divinity from the last decade of the reign of Queen Victoria until well into the new century." This is due, he points out, at least partially to the influence of those theologians who published the volume of essays entitled *Lux Mundi* (1889). These men were latter-day Tractarians, and thus they retained "the sense of the moral significance of every Christian dogma, the feeling for the mysterious in religion and for the unity of sacrament and Incarnation." But they were also interested in making the faith relevant to the contemporary mind, so they described their aim in the preface as "to put the Catholic faith in its right relation to modern intellectual and moral problems." Their incarnationalism thus became a way to see spiritual significance in the world: "He who became Incarnate is the Logos who has been at work in the whole created world, in nature and in man, in art and in science, in culture and in progress. . . ." And Archbishop Temple stands in this tradition when he writes that the world is a series of strata from matter to human spirit to the ultimate Reality, which is God. It follows that the entire universe is revelatory or sacramental: "the world, which is the self-expressive utterance of the Divine Word, becomes itself a true revelation, in which . . . what comes is not truth concerning God, but God Himself."[53] Such a universalized sacramentalism lies behind much Christian Criticism.

Also central for recent Christian Criticism is the study of image and metaphor, as we noted in the discussion of the New Critics. In holding that poetry is basically metaphoric, the New Critics were attempting to establish poetry as a viable means of human discourse against the philosophers of the logical positivist camp, such as Bertrand Russell, A.J. Ayer, or Ludwig Wittgenstein, who looked at empirically verifiable scientific language as alone having meaning, dismissing poetry as meaningless or merely subjective and emotive. The New Critics, most of whom were theological conservatives, were also concerned to establish poetry's independence from religion, which is revealed. But since the logical positivists usually dismissed religion along with poetry, it was difficult to defend one without the other; this is evident in the writings of those who have asserted the significance of nonscientific language: philosophers like Ernst Cassirer or Mercea Eliade or Susanne Langer, critics like Philip Wheelwright, and theologians like Reinhold Niebuhr or Paul Tillich.

The treatment of image and symbol is hardly to be separated from the treatment of myth, which has grown out of the cultural anthropologists' research into the significance of ritual and magic, the Freudian study of dream symbolism, and the Jungian investigation of archetypes. Biblical studies as well as literary criticism have utilized the concept of myth; so it is not surprising that some contemporary Christian Criticism is in this area.

CHAPTER TWO

THE RELATIONSHIP OF RELIGIOUS TRUTH TO ARTISTIC TRUTH

Natural Theology and Christian Criticism

Once it is decided (1) that art is worthy of consideration as something more than the sinful product of a depraved race, and (2) that art is not interchangeable with religion, the Christian who would deal with art must establish what is for him a satisfactory relationship between faith and art. Since Christianity and art both make "truth claims," in what way is the Christian, who is committed primarily to the truth of his faith, going to find legitimate truth residing in art? Most Christian Critics avowedly or implicitly draw on the tradition of natural theology, and view art as "natural" truth. Some recent theology, however, collapses the ancient category of the supernatural into the natural, and to Tillich and his followers such theological dualism is simply irrelevant.

Natural theology has had a checkered career in the twentieth century. For Roman Catholics its importance was asserted by the First Vatican Council in 1870, which proclaimed that "Holy Mother Church holds and teaches that God . . . may certainly be known by the natural light of human reason, by means of created things."[1] This is a reaffirmation of the Thomistic synthesis of the natural and the supernatural, a scheme which provides for the investigation of the natural along Aristotelian lines.

Not explicitly labeled natural theology but finding its sanction in the Neo-Thomist system is the work of Jacques Maritain, the foremost modern Roman Catholic aesthetician. Maritain declares, following the Schoolmen, that art "is what Aristotle called an *hexis*, in Latin a *habitus*, an inner quality or stable and deep-rooted disposition that raises the human subject and his natural powers to a higher degree of vital information and energy." Art is not a theological or moral virtue but "a virtue of the practical intellect— that particular virtue of the practical intellect which deals with the creation of objects to be made."[2] It is not a moral virtue because morality has to do with man's free will and action whereas art has to do with the making of a work.

Maritain also writes of poetry and theology, making a distinction between art and poetry: "By Art I mean the creative or producing, work-making activity of the human mind. By Poetry I mean, not the particular art which consists in writing verses, but a process both more general and more primary: that intercommunication between the inner being of things and the inner being of the human Self which is a kind of divination (as was realized in ancient times; the Latin *vates* was both a poet and a diviner). Poetry, in this sense, is the secret life of each and all of the arts." The key to poetry, in Maritain's sense, is creative intuition, which is "an obscure grasping of [the poet's] own Self and of things in a knowledge through union or through connaturality which is born in the spiritual unconscious, and which fructifies only in the work." Creative intuition is a function of what Aquinas called the "Illuminating Intellect . . . an inherent part of each individual's soul and intellectual structure, an inner spiritual light which is a participation in the uncreated divine light, but which is in every man, through its pure spirituality ceaselessly in act, the primal quickening source of all his intellectual activity."[3]

Does this line of thinking lead Maritain to the Crocean conclusion that religion, as well as art, is the product of the imagination? On the contrary, he takes every pain to emphasize that art and poetry have to do with nature rather than grace. Regarding artistic inspiration, he writes: "There exists a real inspiration, coming not from the Muses, but from the living God, a special movement of the natural order, by which the first intelligence, when it pleases, gives the artist a creative movement superior to the yardstick of reason, and which uses, in superrelevating them, all the rational energies of art; and whose impulse, moreover, man is free to follow or to vitiate." He also warns against the romantic tendency to claim that poetry seizes the absolute: "Poetry (like metaphysics) is spiritual nourishment; but of a savor which has been created and which is insufficient. There is but one eternal nourishment. Unhappy you who think yourselves ambitious, and who whet your appetites for anything less than the three Divine Persons and the humanity of Christ."[4]

Theology, then, according to Maritain, stands in a twofold relationship to art and poetry: on the one hand, it must warn them of their limitations; on the other hand, it must reassure them of their ultimately divine origin: "By showing us where moral truth and the genuine supernatural are situate, religion saves poetry from the absurdity of believing itself destined to transform ethics and life, saves it from overweening arrogance. But in teaching man the discernment of immaterial realities and the savor of the spirit, in linking poetry and art itself to God, it protects them against cowardice and self-abandonment, enables them to attain a higher and more rigorous idea of their essential spirituality, and to concentrate their inventive activity at the fine point thereof."[5]

Several other Roman Catholics writing on the relation of religion and art also use the idea of the "natural" in the Thomistic sense. But I have found none who is able to bring the criteria of supernatural revelation to bear on literature without diminishing its natural integrity, which Maritain is so careful to maintain. Harold C. Gardiner, S.J., for many years literary critic for the Jesuit weekly *America*, often displays the extreme occasionalism of the periodical writer, as well as a narrow sectarianism which, unhappily, is characteristic of many of the older Roman Catholic critics. He does, though, advance the interesting notion that some fiction deals with the "natural" virtues of faith, hope, and charity.[6] Natural hope is "an anticipation of good for ourselves and for others." It is related to natural faith because "if a character in a story engages in the struggle which manifests the fact that he hopes, he does it because he has a certain amount of faith in himself, a certain amount of trust and self-confidence. The reader likewise will conceive a certain amount of trust in the character." In the works of the writers Gardiner admires (those he cites are Roman Catholics), he sees "natural charity," which is present when "the author sees as he writes that the moral world and the supernatural world are things to be loved." It will also be present in the author's attitude to his characters, who though they may be weak will nevertheless be at least potential objects of love. Now the author may not be conscious of the implicitly religious dimensions of his writing, but this fact does not militate against the fundamental religiousness of his art. For in addition to the conscious purpose the author has in mind (the *finis operantis*), there is "an intrinsic finality, a goal inherent in the work itself (*finis operis*), and this will be operative whether the author thinks of it or intends it or not." This second sort of purpose is present because art, imitating the actions of men, is inevitably concerned with the moral atmosphere which, in the widest sense, "envelopes man in his relationship to God."[7] Regrettably, Gardiner's practice is not always as subtle as his theory, for his practical criticism too often expends itself railing against the evil "naturalists" among twentieth-century writers, and even descends to a defense of censorship.[8]

Martin Turnell advances his own version of art as being within the province of nature rather than grace, stressing the distinction: "History shows that art is a spontaneous activity. Even in the most primitive societies we find man taking a delight in reproducing the world about him, and his attempts, however crude, have always found willing spectators. In fact art satisfies . . . some *natural* need in man." But, he says, we must keep in mind "that man has both *religious* and *emotional* needs, and that one *activity* can never be a *substitute* for another without doing violence to his nature, without ending in unhappiness and disillusionment." Because it is natural, the poetic experience is more universal than Catholicism; drawing on Eliot's concept of tradition, Turnell can therefore write that "the great poet is not an individual, but a member of a hierarchy of dead and living poets. Thus the experience we get from major poetry is not something that happened to an individual, it is something that happened to human nature." Therefore "whether Catholics or not, we are bound to be affected by what happened to our human nature in Shakespeare or in Baudelaire."[9]

Still, Turnell holds that the most effective vantage point for the critic is Catholicism. His reason, curiously enough, is that Catholicism, unlike narrow materialism, is the most inclusive philosophy available. Here Turnell apparently considers materialism a distinct, though narrower, rival to Catholicism. Elsewhere, however, his position seems to be that Catholicism is the only coherent view, the work of an unbeliever presenting only unrelated moods. But he claims to be wary of strict dogmatizing: "the first thing a Catholic must realize," he writes, "is that in the literary order dogma must never be applied dogmatically. To assume that only certain forms of experience are valuable or that only those experiences are valuable which are completely Christian, is to condemn oneself to sterility at the outset. They may be the most valuable experiences, but they are by no means the only valuable experiences." Furthermore, he insists that "the critic must approach works of art as works of art, not as sociological treatises. The clue is not the poet's beliefs or his morality, but his style."[10]

A similar theory is advanced by Arthur Machen, whose criterion for literature is that it accord with Catholic dogma, though he adds that no literal adherence to Christianity is necessary, because "from the literary standpoint, Catholic dogma is merely the witness, under a special symbolism, of the enduring facts of human nature and the universe.[11] I suspect that this is going about as far as a Roman Catholic can go in stressing natural truths (though Machen never uses the Thomistic categories) over against revelation.

Anglicans lack the authority of a Vatican pronouncement, but one could point to Hooker and the Caroline Divines, to the seventeenth-century Cambridge Platonists, and to Paley's *Evidences* and *Natural Theology* to indicate a continuous preoccupation with various aspects of natural theology in their tradition. It is perhaps the importance of natural theology in Anglicanism which throws into stark relief the paucity of natural theology in twentieth-century theology as a whole, and which has occasioned calls for its revival. The most influential of these appeals is H.E. Root's "Beginning All Over Again." The title in itself is indicative of the fact that natural theology, which Root defines as "that body of knowledge which may be obtained by human reason alone without the aid of revelation," is today "the sick man of Europe." He notes the older natural theologies of Saint Thomas and Descartes, the challenges to the possibility of natural theology by Hume and Kant, and the modern denials of natural theology by "the fashionable biblical theology" (presumably the Barthian school) and "the fashionable analytic philosophy." Given this history, it is no surprise that natural theology is in poor health. But the point of Root's essay is that it must not be allowed to die, for unless the theologians resume contact with nontheological modes of thought they will cut themselves off definitively from the intellectual world of all nontheologians—something the Church in a post-Christian era cannot afford to do, for the result is likely to be a dangerously irrational fideism. The erosion since Kant of the older natural theology, however, makes necessary a new understanding of it in the light of modern thought. At this point Root cites with approval recent theological attempts to deal with analytic philosophy. Then (and this is particularly interesting) he closes the essay with a plea to the new natural theologian, for the health of theology, to take especial cognizance of the contemporary imagination as it exhibits human nature in literature.[12]

In fact, knowledge of literature is seen as the *propaedeutic* to a viable natural theology. Root writes: 'Before natural theology can begin to function in our day it must have a sense of the inwardness of the lives we lead.

Where do we look now for faithful, stimulating, profound accounts of what it is to be alive in the twentieth century? The inevitable answer to that question carries a judgment. We look to the poet or novelist or dramatist or film producer. In creative works of art we see ourselves anew, come to understand ourselves better and come into touch with just those sources of imagination which should nourish efforts in natural theology." Twenty-two years earlier, Michael Roberts voiced a similar suggestion in *Theology*: "The purposes which poetry can serve in relation to theology and morality are these: it can render more vivid and more urgent the realities on which rational theology rests, it can put moral truths in a persuasive and effective form, and it can help to resist that narrowing of sympathy and coarsening of sentiment which is itself immoral."[13] The tone of Roberts's article is much more conservative than that of Root; it also shows the influence of the *Scrutiny* school on the critics who wrote in *Theology*.

Going still further back in time, we see that definite use is made of natural theology by one of the earliest theologians to take up the question of literature for the Christian. A.H. Strong, an American and a Baptist, states: "the great poets, taken together, give united and harmonious testimony to the fundamental conceptions of natural religion, if not to those of the specifically Christian scheme."[14] It would be difficult to find a contemporary Baptist expressing such confidence in natural theology.

Amos N. Wilder, who wrote the first really serious and systematic examination of the relationship between theology and literature, also makes use of the doctrine. He reviews the age-old denigration of poetry by religionists as well as the modern emphasis on poetic autonomy, and nevertheless arrives at the position that even the poets who consciously exclude religious elements from their work "in the ultimate experience that animates the poem find themselves on religious ground." He defends this assertion on the grounds of natural theology, arguing that the theory that poetic and religious experience are closely related is based on the assumption of "a natural or universal revelation which has its expression in either art or religion. Religion must therefore include the witness of poetry among its evidences."[15]

A strong call for a Christian Criticism based on natural theology is voiced as well by the distinguished literary scholar Frederick A. Pottle, who confesses that as Protestants and Evangelicals we need a clearer idea of natural theology, and specifically of the relation of revealed to natural knowledge. But since it is held by many philosophers and theologians that "*all* arrival at truth is by a species of revelation," Pottle suggests the alternative terms *special* and *general* revelation. Under the rubric of general revelation he puts not only the exercise of human reason but the exercise of the imagination as well: both are "religious." Religion in the broadest sense includes both kinds of revelation, for it is "the total response of man to the fullness of Christ."[16]

Another perspective on literature from the standpoint of natural theology is provided in a brief warning by Nathan A. Scott, Jr., to those who would imperially impose a ready-made Christian system onto the study of literature: "The Christian scholar . . . had better not come prancing into the forums of our cultural life with a Christian system of aesthetics or with a Christian system of psychology or with a Christian system of anything else. For the world is one, the same for the Christian as for all other men of whatever persuasion: if Christ is truly the *Logos*, then he is witnessed to in all apprehensions of truth, whether they occur within a framework of Christian concern or not." Logos theology, says the church historian Williston Walker, is at least as old as Philo of Alexandria (B.C. 20–A.D. 42?), who identified the Old Testament Wisdom (e.g. in Proverbs) with the Logos which "flows out of the being of God Himself, and is the agent not merely through whom God created the world, but from whom all other powers flow."[17] The Church identified the Logos with Christ the source of all truth as the basis for the development of natural theology.

Protestantism, however, both Reformed (Calvinist) and Lutheran, has always harbored strong suspicion of natural theology or the idea of natural law, stressing that the Fall has perverted man's loyalties so that he tends not to perceive natural truth or act on the basis of natural goodness. It is therefore somewhat of a surprise to read a modern Lutheran, David Baily Harned, appealing to natural law on the grounds that God is the source of all creation, and that rejection of natural law has perennially been accompanied by a gnostic attitude to the world. He centers his argument, however, on Christology rather than rational philosophy: "Approached from the vantage point of the gospel, creation means grace. It is the promise freely offered to Abraham and fulfilled in Christ which is the meaning and goal of creation." This is the promise of redemption, by which Christ, the Second Person of the Godhead, was the image of the perfect and fulfilled man before the creation of the universe. His life and gospel provide the standard of human life, of faith and love-of-neighbor tending towards what Harned labels "community." He defines the natural as "[w]hatever contributes to the design of this Lord for community, no matter whether undertaken in faith or ignorance of the Christ. Whatever corrupts and erodes such life together is the unnatural."[18]

Art comes into the picture as it is conducive to this community, and Harned suggests several possibilities. The historian Johan Huizinga wrote that art was a form of play; agreeing with this, Harned observes that art as play directs human competitiveness into ordered, structured expression.

Also, art protects against that which threatens community. Even the most pessimistic, bleak work of literature, for example, contains implicit assumptions about human experience of the world—its specificities and concreteness—and of other people as well. Furthermore, it contains assumptions about the coherence and worth of this experience which testify, however obliquely, to human community. The very fact that art is intelligibly formed expression witnesses to the possibility that human experience can be meaningfully organized, clarified, and shared. Finally, by clarifying and structuring experience, the artist in words helps to "redeem" language from becoming stereotyped and jargonized, from becoming the excuse for shoddy and unscrutinized emotions or the victim of the propagandist and the salesman. All these perversions of language are unnatural, for they get in the way of genuine human encounters and relationships which contribute to community.

Theology of Culture and Christian Criticism

Also associated with the habit of natural theology, though perhaps more prominent among those Christian Critics whose background is Protestant and therefore less sympathetic to the traditional term, is the theory that art is significant to the Christian as an indication of the cultural situation which must be understood if the gospel is to be made relevant to man today.

During the 1930s at least two theologians, one German and one American, began to take seriously the contemporary culture. The German, Paul Tillich, was in the next thirty years to become very important for the theology of Christian Criticism. In his early work, he analyzed the twentieth-century revolt from capitalism, scientism, and rationalism, and drew heavily on the artistic life of the times while doing so, because, as he put it: "Art indicates what the character of a spiritual situation is; it does this more immediately and directly than do science and philosophy for it is less burdened by objective considerations." In painting, symbolism, mysticism, and expressionism have destroyed realism and impressionism; but a "a new realism" is on the rise, which has exposed the "demonism" in the present society and promises to develop into a "belief-ful realism." H. Richard Niebuhr, himself a theologian of note, explains that belief-ful realism refuses to idealize or romanticize; instead it "sees the world with the sober eyes of the scientist or realistic artist, accepting it at the same time as symbolic of the eternal and unconditioned source of all meaning and ground of all being."[19] Here are the seeds of Tillich's later theology of art, but for the moment the emphasis is historical.

The American, Halford E. Luccock, recognizes that modern literature, literature by Americans, is worthy of extended theological notice. He does not attempt a systematic Christian aesthetic; rather, he regards literature "as the expression of life, the symptoms of the moods of the time, its health and its sickness, its despairs and its hopes; the wrist of the common body of life, as it were, where we can count its heartbeats. All of these things are primary concerns of religions." Unlike many other Christians, Luccock does not flail out wildly at "decadent" modern naturalism. Instead, he defends such novelists as Dreiser and Sherwood Anderson as honestly portraying modern dilemmas, and chooses to attack what remains of the older romantic optimism, which, paradoxically, has elements in it of puritanical repressiveness (he has read H.L. Mencken, it is clear). On the other hand, he is depressed by T.S. Eliot's *The Waste Land* and the work of Edwin Arlington Robinson, Fitzgerald, Dos Passos, Hemingway, Faulkner, Huxley, and Joyce as evidencing "the gray twilight of religious faith." He sees the characters in the novels by these writers to be, as Joseph Wood Krutch demonstrated in *The Modern Temper*, incapable of tragedy. They are also incapable of any deep personal relationships.[20] Still, Luccock can infer a "search for God" from such works as O'Neill's *Lazarus Laughed* and Marc Connolly's *Green Pastures* even if the traditional labels are no longer affixed to man's spiritual longings. Many of these themes will be echoed by later Christian Critics.

As was noted above, the first individual to undertake a systematic program of "Christian Criticism" was Amos N. Wilder. In a later examination of such post-World War I writers as Robinson Jeffers, D.H. Lawrence, Yeats, and Eliot, Wilder defers to the New Critics by agreeing that only aesthetic criteria are proper for judging strictly poetic merit; but poetry reveals also "basic viewpoints or convictions." Furthermore, the new poets are to be studied by the modern Christian because they "are apt to be the first to register the profound tides that move society and culture. They are the sensitive ones that first register and react to changes in the climate."[21] The metaphysical crises they record, Wilder contends, can only be ignored by the Church if that institution hides its head in a fusty orthodoxy, and if it ignores the present workings of the Holy Spirit in opening the eyes of moderns to contemporary perdition and to the vicissitudes of the new faiths men have turned to upon the collapse of the traditions.

Wilder subsequently fills in historical background, discussing the primitive and biblical relationship of religion and poetry, and tracing the influences of Christianity (and especially Protestantism) on British poetry since Milton and on American poetry since the Puritans. He also describes the special problems for modern Catholic, Protestant, and "secular" literature: the Catholic is caught in the rigidity of post-Tridentine theology; the Protestant lacks a coherent body of symbolism; and the secular poet is in danger of making his secularism his religion without realizing it. He rejects as well the "Plea for Christian Discrimination," pointing out the shortcomings of the *Theology* group but also outlining possible directions for a Christian aesthetic with a Protestant orientation. Protestant freedom, because of the lack of a permanently constraining theological system, can "effect new combinations of grace and nature,"[22] and allows the Protestant critic to see grace "incognito," hidden or indirectly present in the work of such writers as Robinson Jeffers and William Faulkner.

Thus far the critics cited seem to retain something of the traditional distinction betweeen the supernatural and the natural, the sacred and the secular—though with Luccock and Wilder the borderline is becoming less clear and less important. For Tillich such distinctions are even less applicable; what is important for him is the distinction between the "preliminary concern" and "ultimate concern" (which is his definition of religion). This is not the old sacred-secular division into two mutually exclusive or complementary spheres, for Tillich writes that "the holy embraces itself and the secular, precisely as the divine embraces itself and the demonic. Everything secular is implicitly related to the holy. It can become the bearer of the holy. The divine can become manifest in it. Nothing is essentially and inescapably secular. Everything has the dimension of depth, and in the moment in which the third dimension is actualized, holiness appears. Everything secular is potentially sacred, open to consecration." It is the dimension of depth which constitutes the religious character. Another way Tillich expresses this is by saying that through his culture man expresses his unconditioned concern, his "total surrender," his "infinite passion and interest."[23]

Thus he describes religion and culture as inseparable: "As the substance of culture is religion, so the form of religion is culture. There is only this difference, that in religion the substance which is the unconditioned source and abyss of meaning is designated, and the cultural forms serve as symbols for it; whereas in culture the form, which is the conditioned meaning is designated, and the substance, which is the unconditioned meaning becomes perceptible only indirectly throughout the autonomous form." One implication of this is that art becomes important for the theologian: "Pictures, poems, and music can become objects of theology, not from the point of view of their aesthetic form, but from the point of view of their power of expressing some aspects of that which concerns us ultimately, in and through their aesthetic form."[24]

Given this existential dimension of human culture, what then is the theologian's task? Tillich's criticism resembles the "reading of culture" proposed by such critics as Wilder; it arises out of Tillich's "method of correlation," by which the theological method is fitted to problems of culture. The analysis of the human condition, he writes, must take into account man's cultural expressions in all their forms, including poetry, drama, and the novel; in fact, the entire theological enterprise must be guided by the direction of man's so-called secular life. Furthermore, in his art criticism Tillich uses terms that have been picked up by some of the Christian Critics of literature, and he also makes what amount to aesthetic judgments.[25]

For Tillich the aesthetic norm, as we have seen earlier, is "realism," to which he contrasts two other artistic attitudes which he finds inadequate: "idealism" he considers an escape from reality in an attempt to transcend it; "self-limiting realism" (positivism, pragmatism, empiricism) goes to the opposite extreme and denies transcendence. Belief-ful or "self-transcending" realism combines the two extremes: it "tries to point to the spiritual meaning of the real by using its given forms." This preference lies behind his specific praise of expressionism in "Protestantism and Artistic Style." Expressionism both deals with reality and transcends its literalness. It radically transforms ordinarily experienced reality, expressing through selected elements of it the "'dimension of depth' in the encountered reality, the ground and abyss in which everything is rooted." Tillich sees this expressive depth as the hallmark of all great periods of religious art, for it is this style ("style" is defined as "that which points to a self-interpretation of man") rather than the presence of traditionally "religious" subject matter or a certain form which is significant for a theology of culture.[26]

As a concrete example of truly "religious" art, Tillich considers Picasso's "Guernica," which he calls "a great Protestant painting" because it emphasizes human finitude, mortality, and bondage to destructive forces. Such a portraiture of man, he says, demands acceptance of the Reformation paradox that "it is man in anxiety, guilt, and despair who is the object of God's unconditional acceptance." The fact that "Guernica" expresses the human situation so courageously implies that, in a sense, the human situation is thereby transcended, for "he who can bear and express guilt shows that he already knows about 'acceptance-in-spite-of.' He who can bear and express meaninglessness shows that he experiences meaning within his desert of meaninglessness."[27] Other critics, such as Luccock and Wilder, praised artists who faced modern man's plight honestly, but Tillich assigns this honesty a particular theological value.

Roger Hazelton sees two stages in the modern encounter between religion and the arts. The first, exemplified by Tillich, is criticism which documents man's present alienation from God. The second, more genuinely a dialogue with the modern arts, deals with issues such as the nature of tragedy; the significance of words, images, and myth; the quest for a Christian poetics; and the relation of imagination to belief.[28] The man who is probably the most important Christian Critic on the present scene, Nathan A. Scott, Jr., has written criticism characteristic of both "stages". Accordingly, his name will come up in connection with all the major themes of Christian Criticism, for he is without a doubt the most versatile and prolific writer in the field.

Scott's own poetics begins with a thorough review of "the modern mind": the history of secularization and the discrediting of the imagination by a positivism which he traces from Hobbes to the present linguistic analysts. He then reviews modern literary criticism, especially the New Criticism, which has insisted on the poem as an independent, nonreferential structure. But if a poem "neither points outward toward the world nor inward toward the poet's subjectivity, if it is wholly self-contained and cut off from the general world of meaning, why then it would seem that nothing really can be said about it all." Trying to free criticism from such a narrow impasse, Scott turns to a discussion of the creative process. He mentions Maritain's analysis of creative intuition, which involves a double activity: "the poet permits himself to be invaded by the reality of 'Things' and . . . he himself seeks to invade the deepest recesses of his own subjectivity." The merit of Maritain, Scott observes, is that he stresses the prime importance of what Scott terms poetic vision, "the act of consent which the poet gives to some fundamental hypothesis about the nature of existence which itself in turn introduces structure and coherence for him into the formless stuff of life itself." Therefore he can say that the literary work "is *oriented* toward the world of existence that transcends the work—and the work is *oriented* by the *vision*, by the *belief*, by the *ultimate concern* of which it is an incarnation: its orientation, that is to say, is essentially religious." Therefore criticism, too, must be theological, he concludes. But it is literary as well, he insists, reminding us that he has learned from the New Critics that "whatever it is that *orients* a work of literary art or that constitutes the *ultimate concern* that it embodies is something that will disclose itself in the ways in which the writer brings the resources of language into the service of his project."[29]

His terminology in these passages indicates that Scott has drawn not only on Maritain but also on Tillich to provide theological background for his own critical theory. Furthermore, he brings to his aid the philosophy of Martin Buber, the modern Jewish writer whose influence has been profound among existentially minded Christian thinkers. Buber distinguishes between two modes of confronting experience: in terms of "the world of 'I,' which comprises all the things that we experience and use, all the things that we arrange and organize and manipulate; this, primarily, the world of science and technology"; and in terms of "the world of 'Thou,' . . . here we are addressed, and we must respond; and thus the individual is no longer the sole arbiter of the situation, since it includes, besides himself, another independent center of intelligence and volition—and between these two the relation is that of an *I* to a *Thou* who is not to be experienced or used but who is to be *met* in relation."[30] The world of "I-Thou" involves love; and in this way the "I" becomes a truly human person instead of an isolated self. Scott proceeds to say that Buber has elaborated a principle relevant not only to metaphysics and ethics but also to aesthetics: the good poem moves us to a relational experience with the world incarnated within it by the poet's vision of Creation. To be moved to contemplate created things is to avoid the "angelism" which attempts to escape the concretion of existence and fly to the absolute idea. Against this temptation the Christian Critic calls for affirmation of Creation, of finite existence.[31]

The end of criticism, according to Scott, will be evaluation of the work of art under consideration. After the Christian Critic has ascertained the nature of the poetic vision incarnated in the style of the poem, he will judge it in terms of comprehensiveness, coherence, and depth. Then he will "demonstrate the respects in which the inadequacy of a writer's metaphysic or religion is a factor making for the *aesthetic* failure of his poem or novel, in so far as it fails to provide an appropriate support for his sensibility and an adequate myth for the interpretation of the human story." He is not to sit in judgment on a work of art armed with the standards of some dogmatic orthodoxy, though Scott admits that the Christian will take note of "the extreme difficulty that a writer must face who does not finally view the human tragedy in the light of the Cross."[32] In other words, he will not attempt to palm off his criticism as neutral or objective—which would be either deception or unexamined naiveté.

Secular Theology and Christian Criticism

The critics discussed thus far have in some way looked at art from a theological perspective; they have entered into what Tillich would call a dialogue between Christianity and art. But increasingly in recent years the role of religious presuppositions has declined for some critics, who have become more open to man's culture and at the same time more critical of religion. If we were to retain the classical division between the natural and the supernatural or the secular and the sacred, it would be the former which we would see looming more and more significantly while the latter is questioned, and finally totally abandoned by the "radical theologians."

This movement to the "world" was adumbrated by some of the Christian Critics of literature while Protestant theology as a whole was dominated by the shallow romantic optimism which prevailed until World War II, and later, by the opposite tendency, pessimistic, world-denying Barthianism. Meanwhile Christian Critics were going outside theology and the Church, searching for the prophetic voice. Luccock accused a complacent Protestantism of being puritanical, especially about sex; devoted to "a viciously unwholesome preoccupation with the wholesome"; and sold out to a rosy, laissez-faire optimism. The remedy he recommends is the realistic fiction of Dreiser and Sinclair Lewis; this current literature was not so much concerned with attacking God as it showed no interest in or awareness of him. But to react negatively to this neglect would be only parochial. We must expand our definition of religion; if we do, we discover many writers dealing with experiences traditionally important for religion. Luccock sees as a hopeful sign the fact that "at last the Christian religion has broken its theological jail. It is loose in the world. Nothing human is foreign to it."[33]

Amos N. Wilder goes a step further. His eyes are focused on the writers of "contemporary perdition" and the cultists of irrational faiths that are alternatives to Christianity (e.g., Robinson Jeffers and D.H. Lawrence). But like Luccock, it is to writers, especially the secularists and the agnostics, rather than to the Church that Wilder turns when he wants ethical perceptiveness. He defends Yeats's rejection of the Christian option on the grounds that too often Christianity denies the world with which the artistic vision must deal: "For the poets the scandal of Christ is his asceticism. The very medium of their art as poets; indeed, the very element of their experience as men, is the gamut of human living, emotions, drama. 'Man's resinous heart' and the loves, loyalties, the pride, the grief it feeds—these are the stuff of poetry and the sense of life. And the Cross lays its shadow on this; it draws away all the blood from the glowing body of existence and leaves it mutilated and charred in the hope of some thin ethereal felicity." As a result of this situation the Protestant artist (Wilder is here adopting Tillich's "Protestant Principle" of constant self-criticism and reformation) is allied to the creative unrest in our society: "Protestantism as a creative tradition is today in many respects like a river that has gone underground. But it gives signs of itself especially among the secularists, and even in the blasphemers." What theological interpretation is to be placed on this strange new state of affairs? Wilder's response is to affirm secularity. The irrelevance of much institutional religion "has involved the 'world' in a peculiar responsibility for the faith and in a process of travail with the faith, in considerable measure apart from the guidance of the church."[34]

Hans Egon Holthusen goes even further and identifies the Christian poet in our day not only with blasphemy but with godlessness: "Can anyone deny that the Christian poet shares in the suffering from the godlessness, theologically speaking, of our epoch, or that he profits, aesthetically speaking, from the same godlessness? The Christian poet, like the secular writers of the present age, is given a freedom and a responsibility to 'define his own reality.' He too feels a melancholy emancipation of spirit, the dizzy free-floating freedom of the godless. Whatever is human moves him, but it does not shock him. He must grapple with it."[35]

The movement from the sacred to the secular which was evident in Christian Criticism during the forties and fifties became a major tendency of theology, especially what was called "radical" theology, in the mid-sixties.

Three American "radical" theologians, Gabriel Vahanian, Thomas J.J. Altizer, and William Hamilton, all contribute their own reevaluation of Christianity in the modern world, but they are united in proclaiming what Nietzsche in *The Gay Science* called "the death of God" and in finding ample documentation in imaginative literature for the thesis that the old notions of God are no longer viable. Gabriel Vahanian is the most conservative of the three; he contends, buttressing his argument from the works of Graham Greene, Georges Bernanos, Samuel Beckett, Dostoyevsky, Kafka, and other writers, that the death of God is a "cultural phenomenon" which liberates us from the old sacral-mythological world-view and perhaps paves the way for a new clarification of the concept of God as the "Wholly Other."[36]

Thomas J.J. Altizer goes further than describing the death of God as a cultural phenomenon: for him it is "an historical event . . . God has died in our cosmos, in our history, in our *Existenz*." Indeed, he constructs an elaborate system in which secularity and immanence are extensions of the Incarnation, of spirit becoming flesh—this descent in turn being part of a larger dialectical movement in which the sacred and the secular are moving towards eventual synthesis. He finds William Blake's "Christian atheism," in which the sacred becomes the secular and the secular sacred, an anticipation of his own theories.[37]

The easiest to understand and also the most pessimistic of the death-of-God theologians is William Hamilton. He cites Camus' *The Plague* and Beckett's *Waiting for Godot* as evidence that modern man no longer experiences faith or hope. Perhaps, he writes elsewhere, love is the only option open, love directed to where Christ is, not as an object of faith but as the "place" to be, standing with the neighbor.[38]

I have included these theologians not as Christian Critics of literature in the usual sense, but because they seem to be turning to the kind of "revelation" afforded by modern literature of the plight of post-Christian man. Nathan A. Scott, Jr. would take an additional step, holding that the death-of-God theologians have gone as far as possible in acceding to an immanentist view of the universe. Scott advises a re-examination of modern literature, for here, he feels, post-Christian man may once again find available the experiences of transcendence and depth which would revivify theology.[39]

Though Scott is subsequently able to dismiss the death-of-God movement as aberrant,[40] changes in the viewpoint of what was written in the 1960s, which hitherto did not provide the models for his generalizations about literature, have forced him to cast about for new theological resources. The expectation that man might, in a positivistic world, discover depth in literature would not seem to be fulfilled. The "new literature," born not out of experiences between the world wars but out of the post-World War II consciousness, must therefore be thought of as "post-modern"—and it has itself become flat, cold, and scientistic. The most articulate apologists for the new literature are a group of French writers: Claude Simon, Michel Butor, Nathalie Sarraute, Marguerite Duras, and Alain Robbe-Grillet. In what amounts to a manifesto for the movement, *For a New Novel*, Robbe-Grillet eschews what he terms the "anthropomorphic" illusion that literary art should order, make sense of experience by creating story lines and characters and interpretations of life. For him and his compatriots "the principle function of literature must be that of trapping us into a kind of radical amazement at the simple thereness of the world and at the stubbornness with which, in its brute factuality, it resists all our traditional habits of ordering and apprehension. Our writers will become *chosistes*, connoisseurs of *things*. . . ."[41]

Inasmuch as such a commitment is a protest against what Scott has previously called "angelism," the temptation to desert the concrete and physical for the abstract and the analytical, it is to be welcomed. But the *chosistes* go further than the "classic moderns"—Faulkner, say, or Lawrence —in that they reject the older assumption that man's encounter with the world can or should take on shape and significance, asserting that only "objective phenomenological description" is to be attempted by the writer. In being so fearful of injecting subjectivism into their writing, Scott charges, they are not giving us "a sense of saturation in historical actuality"; the work of *chosiste* art is likely rather to be only "a skillfully contrived arabesque" or a "complicated geometry."[42]

Although the French practitioners of the *nouveau roman* have constructed the apologetic for the new *alittérature*, rejection of the traditional mythopoeic function of literature is evident, though perhaps less self-conscious, in the "absurdist" drama of Samuel Beckett, Samuel Adamov, and Eugene Ionesco, as well as in the novels of English-language writers Saul Bellow, Joseph Heller, Thomas Pynchon, John Barth, and J. P. Donleavy. The latter are, according to Scott, writers "who do not want greatly to fidget over 'the art of the novel,' for, given their sense of how largely the world itself is indeterminate and astonishing and intractable, their feeling seems to be that one had better write catch-as-catch-can, not bothering overmuch about controlling forms but trusting to the luck of the improviser, throwing the farcical together with the horrific, the arcadian with the gothic, the bitter with the sweet, and allowing one's fictions garrulously to sprawl out into the untidy formlessness of primary existence."[43]

At this point one may wonder whether the secular and death-of-God theologies, combined with the new literature which, in its avoidance of "anthropocentrism," implies not only the death of God but also the death of man for literature, do not bring the whole enterprise of Christian Criticism to an end.[44] Indeed, Scott is forced to look not to a Christian theologian but to the German philosopher Martin Heidegger in an attempt to cope with this recent literary trend.

Ever since Plato's theory of Ideas that are ascertainable to the human intellect, Western thought has, according to Heidegger, located ultimate reality in "what were nothing more than projections of human reason." In recent centuries this "humanization of reality" has led to the so-called technological conquest of nature. The tradition which asserts the human mind and will in order to manipulate reality has lost "attentiveness to the sheer ontological weight and depth of the world." What is desperately needed as a corrective is receptivity to the radiance, the presence of Being, "*Gelassenheit*: submission, abandonment, surrender, acquiescence" to the mystery of things as they are. Heidegger finds such intimacy with the specifications of reality in the poet Hölderlin; Scott notes that a concern with concreteness is apparent in the New Criticism, but that the new literature is willing to surrender, to wait, to "release itself into the openness of Being without violating that openness" by attempting to impose human patterns or meanings. But in the effort to descry theological significance Scott goes further; he regards all reality as sacramental "in the sense that the true identity of everything that exists is considered to reside in its way of showing forth the Mystery of Being." This attitude is also eschatological, for it involves waiting, expectantly, in hope, for the "not yet," sure that "it is indeed in some sense really gracious, that it is worth waiting for."[45]

CHAPTER THREE

THE CREATIVE ACT
IN THEOLOGY AND ART

Having examined in the previous chapters the general problem of a rapprochement between Christianity and artistic literature, in the remaining chapters we shall assume some kind of valid relationship between the two and concentrate on specific areas of concern.

The Doctrine of the Creation

Though in the heyday of the New Criticism speculation about the genesis of poetry was suspect as an attempt to deflect attention from the poem to the poet's intentions or psychology or biography, interest in the creative process never disappeared. Among Christian Critics the doctrines of Creation, Incarnation, and Trinity have been helpful in keeping this interest alive. There has been conjecture at least since Aristotle that somehow artistic creativity was an analogue to cosmic creativity. The *Poetics* uses various forms and derivatives of *poieō* (create) in discussing poetry; it begins with Aristotle's announcing that he will be concerned with "the poetic art [*poiētikēs*] as a whole and its species, the particular capacities of each; how the plots should be constructed if the poetic process [*poiēsis*] is to be artistically satisfactory, and further how many and what kind of parts it has; and all the other questions that belong to the same branch of study." But *poieō* has to do not only with the creation of poetry but with "construction" or "production" in general, and can refer to all kinds of "making": furniture, houses, clothes, etc.[1] However, that Aristotle intended the word to have religious overtones is suggested by at least one modern commentator: "The artist is a *poiētēs*, a 'maker,' and nature is clearly the great Maker, the great 'poet' or artist. The only difference between nature and the human artist is that nature herself makes something out of her own materials, while the human artist makes something out of something else, some materials outside himself, to which he is an external *archē*." If the Christian should object that "Poems are made by fools like me, / But only God can make a tree," Aristotle would answer: "There is a sense in which that is obviously true. But there is a deeper sense in which God or nature and I are just alike: we are both artists. And when I make a poem, God or nature is making it, just as much as when he—or she—is making a tree, only through different agents: through me, and not through the wind, the sun and the rain."[2]

The notion that as God created the universe so the poet creates a little "world" became an aesthetic commonplace during the Renaissance, though (ironically) it appeared among followers of Plato rather than disciples of Aristotle. J.E. Spingarn mentions Scaliger, Tasso, and Sidney in this connection. The idea was echoed by Shaftesbury, who called the poet "a second *Maker*; a just *Prometheus*, under *Jove*. Like that Sovereign Artist or universal Plastick Nature, he forms a *Whole*, coherent and proportion'd in it-self, with due Subjection and Subordinacy of consituent Parts." Later it became important among German writers and was then introduced into modern criticism by Coleridge, in whose work German ideas sometimes appear *verbatim*. In Chapter XIII of the *Biographia Literaria* he writes of the primary imagination that it is "the living Power and prime Agent of all human Perception, and . . . a repetition in the finite mind of the eternal act of creation in the infinite I AM."[3] It is agreed that Coleridge is echoing the German romantics, but his specific source is variously given as Herder, Schelling, and Kant.[4]

Moving now to the modern Christian Critics, we see that the idea of creation is carried even further by the Dutch scholar Gerardus van der Leeuw, who traces the evolution of the arts from the dance, which was the primitive cultic act that included the elements of all the later art forms (drama—the holy play; the pictorial and rhetorical arts—the holy image; architecture—the house of God; music—holy sound). These later art forms subsequently separated and became secularized, and the modern critic is faced with the task of reestablishing the validity of "theological aesthetics." In van der

Leeuw's attempt to do this he remarks that Shaftesbury was correct in claiming that art is a creation, a second world:

> Since Shaftesbury, the poet has been compared to God, or at least to Prometheus, "... under Jupiter. Like that highest artist or universal creative nature, he forms a whole, completely coherent and in itself well formed, with proper order and articulation of its parts."
> Conversely, God is a genius. The Enlightenment and the Age of Genius are right, put in another way than they thought. The artist creates figures, but if he really succeeds, if his work is more than a "work," if it becomes a living creation, then it is not the "creative genius" which accomplishes this miracle, but the creator himself. And the artist is not the proud hero, ... but the humble servant, who with bated breath and trembling excitement recognizes in the work of his hands the image of God.

This is true because, though art arises out of the experience of the artist, it becomes something else: "A poem is not a piece of experience, even if it stands in a particular relationship to experience. It is rather a world newly constructed on the basis of the experience." The independence of art from experience is, in fact, what binds it to religion. Both art and religion involve distancing from experience: art is objectified in form; religion is encounter with the Holy, confrontation with the "Wholly Other," the "Ultimate," which evokes in man awe, dread, and the feeling of smallness. The difference between art and religion is that art has as its "goal of perfection" finite form; whereas to living religion, form (myth, ritual, dogma) is disobedience and sin.[5]

Van der Leeuw also views poetic creation from a strictly Christian vantage point, where it is not "a stationary bringing-into-being, but a pledging of one's life for what is created." To the Christian, God created the world out of love, which fact is corroborated by the gift of Christ to the world. Similarly, every artist can testify that "love is the element in which one's own life and the work of art are united." The artist forgets himself, loses himself in the subject of his work in an attitude which is analogous to religious service and sacrifice.[6]

The doctrine of Creation, understood in the light of the Russian Orthodox tradition, plays an important part in the thinking of Nicolas Berdyaev, the most well-known modern exponent of Eastern Orthodoxy. Berdyaev's philosophy is strongly eschatological—in the sense that he looks towards an increase of freedom which will liberate man from bondage in the world. Creativity is the assertion of this freedom; it is not "mastery over the medium, or the creative product itself; rather it is a flight into the infinite; not an activity which objectifies in the finite but one which transcends the finite towards the infinite. The creative act signifies an *ek-stasis*, a breaking through to eternity."[7] But in this world, the creative impulse often results in cultural expressions such as art works; thus there is a tragic disparity between creativity and art, which are of two worlds.

An understanding of creativity, Berdyaev feels, gives man hope that he will transcend the pessimism and skepticism of the present age. The usual attitude of dead orthodox theology (found in both East and West) is that creativity is sinful, that in the original creative act the divine Creator exhausted his creation and established "absolute quiet and submission." In this view it was only with the fall of man that the *stasis* was broken, that the dynamic re-entered the universe; the end of redemption is to conquer sin and restore the original state of rest. Berdyaev's view is exactly the opposite: "Createdness bears the image and likeness of the Creator, i.e. in createdness itself there are creators. Created nature would be something opposed to creative nature, if in the created there was not evident the image and likeness of the Creator; it is creative nature."[8] The Creator gives man free creative power, and calls upon his creature to continue his "seven days" of Creation.

The notion of creativity is never systematically defined by Berdyaev. He does, however, make a specific connection between creation in a theological sense and art when he writes that "artistic creativeness best reveals the meaning of the creative act. Art is primarily a creative sphere. It is even an accepted expression to call the creative element in all spheres of spiritual activity 'artistic.' A clearly creative attitude towards science, social life, philosophy or morals, we consider artistic. And even the Creator of the world is considered in the aspect of the great artist." Is there, then, a distinction, he asks, between divine and human creativity? Is the artist completely like the Creator? No; for living being, personality, is created only by God, and any attempt by the artist to create living being results only in dead automatons. Furthermore, human creativity, though it is always "a growth, an addition, the making of something new that had not existed in the world before," takes as its materials the world created by God. Man is said to create *ex nihilo* only in the sense that "in every creative conception there is an element of primeval freedom, fathomless, undetermined by anything, not proceeding from God but ascending towards God. God's call is addressed to that abyss of freedom, and the answer must come from it."

But these limits allow no excuse for the old religious orthodoxy which suspects and condemns creative experience. For the artist is expressing no less than the essential direction and purpose of the universe, which is to pass beyond the present finitude (and the religion appropriate to it, which views man as a sinner needing redemption) to "cosmic beauty . . . another kind of being, a higher being which is in process of creation." At present, beauty is only accessible symbolically, but then, cries Berdyaev ecstatically, "the realistic grasp of essential beauty, without the intermediary symbol will be the beginning of the transfiguration of this world, of a new heaven and a new earth."[9]

As a footnote to this discussion of the creative process in the light of the Creation, it might be noted that the artistic impulse in man has been related to the Genesis story of God's giving Adam powers over the universe. Among these powers was the ability to name the creatures. According to van der Leeuw, naming by a word involves the calling forth of an image; this word is "mythos, that is, word and image together. It creates an existence by placing one before our eyes." Objects are thus subjugated through the speaking of a word, and a new world is created for man.[10] Human language is therefore initially an effort to comprehend the world, and to bind it within human understanding.[11] In this connection it is significant that words in formulaic pattern, rhythm, pitch, and order are more potent for this purpose to the primitive mind than what we would call prose; as a result language was originally poetic.

Van der Leeuw's remarks grow out of his research into cultural anthropology, but the relevance today of this kind of theory has been questioned. Delmore Schwartz says that the power to name might have been available "in idyllic and primitive periods" but that the modern poet must resist the misuse and commercialization of language. Schwartz also observes, however, that the poet's acute consciousness of words brings about a strong sensitivity to new levels of meaning which emerge when the older semantic exactness is blurred: thus the misuse is fruitful for the modern poet as well as destructive.[12] Does not this suggest what Schwartz does not seem to mention —that the modern poet is still able to "subjugate" new areas of reality with new words, new names?

Jacques Maritain also objects to the concept of the poet as namer. Poetic knowledge, for him, is "not ordered towards seizing essences" but rather towards expressing the subjectivity of the poet as it is "in active communication with the world." This is because "the poet is not a hierarch who 'calls all things to existence by giving to each thing its proper and everlasting name,' that is to say by knowing it (prophetically) in its essence; he is rather a child who names things by calling them affectionate names, and who makes a paradise with them. They tell him their names only in an enigma, he enters into their games, blindfolded, he plays with them at life and death."[13]

The Doctrine of the Incarnation

Also important to Christian Criticism (though not unrelated to the idea of Creation) is the doctrine of the Incarnation. Given the significance of the Incarnation in Anglican and Roman Catholic theology, one would expect Christian Critics mainly from these traditions to explore its relevance to art and literature; but the fact is that the Incarnation looms large among Protestant critics as well.

A long and detailed discussion of "The Incarnation and Art" by E.J. Tinsley[14] points out that both the Incarnation and art are methods of communication. Quoting Saint Augustine, who said that "The Word is, in a way, the art of Almighty God," Tinsley advances the thesis that the New Testament itself provides evidence for the analogical relationship between the Incarnation and art. Jesus is presented as the unique *eikon* or image of the Father, having the form of ultimate significance; furthermore, the Christian life is a process of being conformed to this image through the action of the Holy Spirit in grace. Thus the Incarnation is not only important as a fact; it is also significant as the method by which God chose to communicate himself. Now the Incarnation is more like the method of art than that of philosophical or scientific statement. Here, as in art, form and content are inseparable, and a variety of response is possible to the one form, Christ. In the early Gospels (Mark, Matthew) Jesus seems deliberately to make himself and his mission mysterious and enigmatic, using images, metaphors, and signs rather than proclaiming himself openly and ostentatiously.[15] Like the dramatic poet, Jesus acted out his mission.[16]

A somewhat different approach is taken by the famous Shakespearean critic G. Wilson Knight, who takes note, as several others have done, that the New Testament is in its own right an art form, the symbolic incarnation or blending by the Divine Artist of suprahistorical truth with the world of history. The Incarnation has other dimensions as well; not only is the New Testament an art form created by the Divine Poet, but its central figure,

Jesus, also corresponds to the art form of the artist: "He is in himself the incarnation the poet accomplishes in art. He creates in his imagination his own poetry and then acts it, making himself protagonist in his own drama."[17]

Other critics, too, have commented on the dramatic implications of the Incarnation. True religion has never been primarily a matter of theoretical propositions, asserts Leicester Bradner. God's dealing with His people in the Old Testament was in terms of specific situations which involved the action of God and human response: Moses and the burning bush, the Exodus, the deliverance of the Law, the stories of David, the tales of the Prophets. The coming of Christ is for the Christian the culmination of this principle: Jesus did not come to preach a new law but to act out the love of God through dramatic example. The New Testament is, moreover, replete with dramatic elements. Scenes in the life of Christ exemplify his teachings (e.g., the encounter with the rich young ruler, and with the tax collector Zacchaeus; the feeding of the five thousand, and the blessing of the little children), and he presents his message largely by parables which are immediate, vivid, and imaginative. Furthermore the Gospels through which we are given the story of Jesus are themselves seen as dramatic in form by Sallie M. TeSelle. Saint Mark presents a human, sympathetic Jesus; his Gospel is comparable to a miracle play and could be acted out in a pantomime emphasizing the various human emotions, such as awe, joy, and compassion. Saint Matthew's Gospel is structured around Jesus as supernatural judge and king who elicits fear; the story is much more stylized, like a morality play. Saint Luke's story is more natural and spontaneous and immediate than the other Synoptics; it stresses the love of Jesus and the gratitude of those who are healed and forgiven by him.[18]

The indirection and enigma of the Incarnation are emphasized by van der Leeuw, who writes from a neo-Calvinist viewpoint and is able, surprisingly enough, to attempt a Christian aesthetic which draws on Barthian theology. With Barth, van der Leeuw emphasizes that we cannot speak of the goodness of creation or of human experience, because man has fallen and the "image of God" in which he was created has been lost. For the Christian there is only the "new creation," in which the image of God appears again— not in "form nor glory" but "emptied into the man of sorrows." Therefore it is only through faith, not metaphysical speculation, that we can hold fast to the image of God: "We cannot command it, we cannot hold it. We can only share in it when we share in the image of God among us, in God in the image of man, in Jesus Christ, who emptied himself and took on the form of a servant." Nature, or human nature as such, is not the image of God, but God has "set up his image among us in the form of the Crucified." We have this form, of death and humiliation; but we have also "the form of resurrected life and of glory." Thus van der Leeuw arrives at a theological basis for his aesthetic: "The doctrine of the image of God includes the entire theological aesthetics or aesthetical theology. In the form of the crucified, humiliated and problematic, yet eternally worthy of worship, lies a judgment, but at the same time also a justification, for all human attempts at creating form. In his triumph lies also the possibility of the miracle which we can never attain, but which is given us as grace: the expression of the holy through the beautiful." Because of this Christological base, van der Leeuw is able to conclude his book with confidence: "It can and must be possible to praise the whole variety of the human world, the glorious multitude of forms of art and religion as revelation of the glory of God, if God himself gave himself to this human world, himself assumed form and moved as man among men."[19]

Here van der Leeuw touches on a major theme among Christian Critics: the Incarnation as the means by which creation—the natural world, concrete human experience—is seen to be good, and of ultimate significance. It is particularly important to establish the goodness of the world of sense, of things, because, as Nathan A. Scott, Jr., points out, there has been a rejection of the world by poets during the past century or so. Citing Allen Tate's essay "The Symbolic Imagination," Scott asserts that the poet "has got to do with the body of this world." Instead, the poet has suffered from the post-Cartesian split between the subjective and the objective, and has shown contempt for finite existence in his pursuit of the infinite "clear and distinct idea"; following Maritain and Tate, Scott labels this tendency angelism.[20] Angelism has evidenced itself in three developments. First, it is seen in mystical gnosis, by which modern poets, from the French Surrealists to Dylan Thomas and Hart Crane, have turned away from the created order in an attempt to directly perceive the Absolute or to create *la poésie pure*, self-sufficient and underived. Second, angelism is evidenced in the abandonment of the mimetic principle; there is thus no perception of the world but only of the consciousness of the perceiver. Third, angelism occurs most radically in the Existentialism set forth by writers such as Sartre, who reduce life to an utterly absurd state of fragmentation and disintegration producing only despair and disgust.

In the face of this trend, it is the task of the Christian Critic to assert once more that literature has to do with finitude, with creation; that the poet is "to glory in our human infirmities and to turn once again to the finite with a sense of wonder and expectancy and with love and a proper adoration." Here Scott brings to bear the philosophical theology of Paul Tillich in order to say to the poet that his dissatisfaction with the finite, inasmuch as it is a yearning for the infinite depth of meaning, itself implies a certain awareness of what Tillich calls the Ground of Being, an awareness ("the condition of being grasped by the power of Being-itself") which Tillich identifies as faith.[21] For the Christian, the Ground of Being is most clearly revealed in the New Being manifested by the New Testament picture of Jesus the Christ. The Incarnation is therefore the prime example of finitude participating in the Unconditional: here the literary imagination possesses the model for piercing to the Ultimate through the depth of existence.

What is only suggested by Scott as a Christian answer to angelism is spelled out by the Jesuit writer William Lynch. Like Scott, Lynch is concerned about various stratagems by which the finite is denied by the imagination: it can scorn creation in favor of a transcendent infinity, or by turning inwards to the self (an example is the "psychologism" practiced by I.A. Richards); it can touch human experience only to recoil in disgust; or it can deny the possibility of a leap into the infinite but at the same time regard the finite as meaningless or absurd. Lynch's own position, on the other hand, is that the infinite (beauty, truth, God) must be approached through a descent into finitude, through the limited and the definite; the model for this descent is the Incarnation.

When Lynch approaches the problem of how ideas or meaning get into the literary work, he sees similar aberrant tendencies. There is, at one extreme, the "univocal" imagination, which reduces or destroys all variety and detail for the sake of unity. Lynch illustrates the univocal pattern by Dr. Rieux in Camus' *The Plague*, by Scobie in Graham Greene's *The Heart of the Matter*, and by Kierkegaard's "aesthetic man." At the other extreme is the "equivocal" imagination, which sees only difference and variety; thus everything is diverse, private, and unrelated to everything else: the example given is André Gide's *acte gratuit*, absolute availability for every novel adventure to the exclusion of all previous experience or commitment. Between these two extremes is the "analogical" imagination, which "insists on keeping the same and the different, the idea and the detail, tightly interlocked in the one imaginative act. As its idea or pattern descends into the images of reality, it adapts itself perfectly to every detail or difference, without ever suffering the loss of its own identity. And the theme is always on the inside of the images. It is always eminently positive and is always creating difference and autonomy." Again Lynch's model is Christological: in Christ the contraries, the One and the Many, are reconciled. The historically unique and differentiated Christ is mysteriously united with the ultimate society of the Church, and this identity of the concrete and the universal is the warrant for the analogical imagination.[22]

Thus, reasons Lynch, it cannot be said, as many modern critics claim, that the imagination is absolutely independent of metaphysics or theology; *la poésie pure* is a chimera, and if complete autonomy is insisted on, the dissociation characteristic of the equivocal imagination will result. How, though, is literature to be approached without running the risk of univocal dogmatizing, which sacrifices the specifics of the poem to an absolute truth? Here Lynch would apply the method of medieval biblical exegesis, which dealt with four levels of meaning: the literal, the allegorical, the anagogical, and the tropological. The integrity of the concrete image is maintained, while, at the same time, if the text is examined in depth it is seen to participate in the dimensions of the universal. The application of the fourfold method of exegesis moves Lynch finally to speculate that there is, besides the partial and inadequate attitudes he has discussed, a "Christian" imagination. In analogy, as we have seen, the "act of existence" descends "into every created form and possibility, adapting itself to every shape and form and difference." But the Incarnation is a new creation, "within which the one, single, narrow form of Christ of Nazareth is in process of giving *its* shape to everything. To think and imagine according to this form is to think and imagine according to a 'Christic' dimension. It would also make every dimension Christic. However, like analogy itself, this would not destroy difference but would make it emerge even more sharply." Lynch has worked out, in the structure of Roman Catholic theology (though he leans more towards the Platonic than the Aristotelian), a strategy similar to the one worked out by Nathan Scott from Tillich's theology. And he provides, I think, the most impressive contribution by a Christian Critic to the discussion of the "concrete universal," and an impressive argument against those who feel that religion is somehow alien to literature and prone to exploit it.[23]

Lynch has not gone unpraised. Nathan A. Scott, Jr. quotes him at length in his discussion of Tillich. Paul Elman, in an essay subtitled "Reality in Contemporary Fiction," also defends the Christian against otherworldliness, citing Tillich and Lynch as well as Erich Auerbach's monumental study *Mimesis*—all examples of criticism which holds that the Incarnation validates concrete existence.[24] And even Sallie M. TeSelle, who usually has little praise for Christian Critics, has kind words for Lynch as a theological theorist, though she disparages his practical criticism of literature. Her own approach is not basically theoretical in orientation, though like Incarnational criticism, it insists on the concreteness of literature. Her perspective is somewhat more pragmatic: literature is valuable as it offers the Christian, "who is called upon to adhere totally to God in spite of the negative powers that appear to rule the world, an understanding of the depth and breadth of powers that his response must embrace if it is to be realistic." This function, however, is not the "program" of literature, which does not need any concerns beyond its own excellence; it is in the will of the individual that this appropriation of literature takes place. The function of literature is for TeSelle pre-ethical: literature is to provide information in depth for the disciple of Christ, to help him to know preparatory to doing. What counts finally is the doing, not the knowing, and Kierkegaard's warnings against aestheticism are repeated. Unlike Auden, though, TeSelle will not go as far as Kierkegaard, for Kierkegaard (like the poets and critics possessed of the "angelic imagination," despite the fact that the similarity is not mentioned by TeSelle) is completely otherworldly, demanding only the response of immediate and total obedience from the Christian while disregarding his circumstances. She insists that the Christian life is "such a mundane, concrete, contemporary business that only an intimate acquaintance with the situation in which we are to do this living out can give us the equipment for a realistic and profound response."[25]

The Doctrine of the Trinity

The critics discussed above draw upon the theology of the Divine Father and the Incarnation of the Divine Son—the first two Persons of the Trinity. But at least two writers have as their model the Trinity itself, which includes as well the Person of the Holy Spirit—the three Persons being mystically One God.

Nicolas Berdyaev links the three "ages" or levels of man's consciousness of God to the Persons of the Trinity. The Old Testament, the age of Law, is identified with God as King, Ruler, Judge—unapproachable and fearsome, before whom man trembled in the dust. The New Testament is the age of Redemption: now man is not only acutely aware of his sinfulness; he sees salvation made possible for him by the grace of a loving Father expressed in the sacrifice of his Son. But redemption never removes man from the position of humble repentance towards the God he has disobeyed. In the realm of obedience, any impulse to creative self-assertion is branded as prideful. This is because orthodox theology, both East and West, has failed to draw adequate anthropological conclusions from the Incarnation, having ignored the meaning of the Holy Spirit and the eschatological promise of the Second Coming.

The New Testament Incarnation of Christ the Logos means that no longer can creativity in the universe be seen solely as the work of the Creator-God; it is now apparent that creation is also of the Son. Unlike many theologians in the West, Berdyaev does not see Christ only as a sojourner among fallen men but as the God-man, through whom man's initial perfection is restored so that now, in some sense, man participates once more in the perfection of the Godhead. Furthermore, God's creativity, to Berdyaev, is not limited to the "seven days" of Genesis but is evident in the Incarnation as well. The Incarnation implies the lifting up of man to Godhead as well as the condescension of divinity to humanity: Christ is the Absolute Man, the Divine Man representing the entire human race before God, and his triumph is the triumph of all men in him. Human creativity is now seen in connection with the divine creativity, and Berdyaev rejoices that "in the consciousness of Christ's incarnation, as a continuation of the creation, there is already implicit man's creative role in the world. It is revealed in God the Son and God the Spirit that God continues His work of creation together with man and his free powers."[26]

For centuries the orthodox theologies of East and West have held man to a passive response to the redemption; however, in the nineteenth and twentieth centuries man has been casting off his former servility and asserting himself. Still theology has clung to the past, leaving man to pervert and destroy himself in the cultural and metaphysical crises of our times with such aberrations as scientism, rationalism, and Marxism. What Berdyaev is attempting to do is devise a theology for the present. In *The Meaning of the Creative Act* he is filled with hope; he is able to proclaim: "Creativeness is the final revelation of the Holy Trinity—its anthropological revelation. This is a consciousness which has never existed in the world—it is being born in our epoch." Creativeness is the third era of Revelation, surpassing the eras of Law and Redemption; it is of the Spirit, and is without external authority or Scripture. And whereas the Law and Redemption were initiated from above, the anthropological revelation will be from man to God. "This world," which weighs down and imprisons, will pass away—this is the Coming of Christ in glory, the Second Coming. As a result, the gap between the making of aesthetic and cultural objects and creativeness will be transcended; "creativity will pass over to cosmic perfection in which man's perfection and the perfection of what he creates will become one," and man will be reborn to a new realm of divine power. This book, written before World War I, now seems dated, especially in its lyric prophecy of the new age of creativity. Later Berdyaev still stresses the apocalyptic hope that the human spirit will transcend the ghastly inhumanity of the present time, though he looks for the victory not in a new age of chronological time but in what he calls "existential time," eternity out of time.[27]

The trinitarian doctrine for Berdyaev has historical and cosmic implications in relation to creativity defined in the broadest sense. But the Trinity also appears as the model for an analysis of poetic creativity as a psychological process by a British medievalist, playwright, and mystery writer, Dorothy L. Sayers.[28] Unlike Berdyaev, who was often condemned as a heretic by his fellow Orthodox and viewed with suspicion by Western Catholics and Protestants, she was an Anglo-Catholic of impeccable orthodoxy. The basis for her discussion is the familiar analogy between the Divine Creator and the human creative artist. But unlike (say) Coleridge, who looked at creative imagination as a "repetition" of eternal creation, Sayers starts from the blatant anthropomorphism of the Genesis story. All our concepts except possibly the most abstract, like numbers, are necessarily based on our experience. Theological statements about God are therefore analogous to statements about human behavior. We speak of God as "King" and "Father," for instance, extrapolating the best elements of royalty and paternity to express aspects of our relationship to God. Similarly, from our knowledge of the human "maker," we fashion the idea of the Divine Maker. The human maker employs the stuff of the universe of which he is a part in order to fashion something that did not exist previously; the Divine Maker is not a part of the universe (which is his creation), and he creates *ex nihilo*. But we could not understand Creation even as imperfectly as we do if we had no experience of human creativity.

The fact that theological language is analogous to human experience is helpful for our understanding of two things which have long been mysterious—so mysterious that they have often been dismissed as incomprehensible: the creative imagination in man, and the dogma of the Trinity. The two can throw light on each other: by looking at the creative imagination in the light of the trinitarian formuation, we can more clearly comprehend its workings; and we can also come to appreciate the Trinity as a concept corresponding to what is recognizably true on the human level rather than impossibly befogged theological nonsense about which any respectable modern man should remain permanently ignorant.[29]

As the germ of her discussion, Sayers introduces the trinitarian structure of the imagination with a passage from one of her liturgical plays, *The Zeal of Thy House.* Saint Michael, in his final speech, says:

For every work [*or act*] of creation is threefold, an earthly trinity to match the heavenly.

First, [*not in time, but merely in order of enumeration*] , there is the Creative Idea, passionless, timeless, beholding the whole work complete at once, the end in the beginning: and this is the image of the Father.

Second, there is the Creative Energy [*or Activity*] begotten of that idea, working in time from the beginning to the end, with sweat and passion, being incarnate in the bonds of matter: and this is the image of the Word.

Third, there is the Creative Power, the meaning of the work and its response in the lively soul: and this is the image of the indwelling Spirit.

And these three are one, each equally in itself the whole work, whereof none can exist without other: and this is the image of the Trinity.[30]

The Idea (the "Father") is the most difficult to grasp, for, like God, it is not directly knowable but, as in the Trinity, ascertainable only as it incarnates itself in the work. In the process of artistic creation the writer refers every word and episode to a pre-existent pattern which thereby becomes conscious. The Idea, like God the Father, is "timeless and without parts or passions, though it is never seen, either by writer or reader, except in terms of time, parts and passion."[31]

The Energy, corresponding to the Son, the Second Person of the Trinity, is "the sum and process of all the activity which brings the book into temporal and spatial existence. 'All things are made by it, and without it nothing is made that has been made.' To it belongs everything that can be included under the word 'passion'—feeling, thought, toil, trouble, difficulty, choice, triumph—all the accidents which attend a manifestation in time . . .

of the eternal and immutable Idea." The relation of the creative poet to his work is viewed as analogous to the relation of the Creator to his Creation; the poet, like God, is both transcendent and immanent. Is it wrong, then, to assert that the poet is merely the sum of his works; this is a kind of artistic pantheism. Neither can we say that the poem has no reality apart from the poet's mind; for once a poem is created it has a separate reality for the reader. On the other hand, artistic deism is also wrong, for a poet cannot express a thought or emotion or character which does not in some way reveal himself. With regard to his created characters, however, the author must avoid two extremes; he must not allow them absolute freedom, or coherence of the work as a whole may be destroyed. Nor must he play the role of autocratic deity, or he will destroy their humanity. Here, in literary terms, is the classic problem of free will and predestination, which ultimately are not contradictory but paradoxically both necessary.

The third Person of the poet's Trinity (analogous to the Holy Spirit) is the Creative Power: "It is the thing which flows back to the writer from his own activity and makes him, as it were, the reader of his own book. It is also, of course, the means by which the Activity is communicated to other readers and which produces a corresponding response in them."[32] Here we have to do with the emotional effect of the poem: its power to call up associations in the mine of the reader, its power to influence his thoughts and behavior.

Finally, as in the Athanasian Creed, "These three are one." Idea, Energy, and Power are intellectually separable but all three are the "real" poem. The poet cannot know the Idea except through its realization in Energy, and he knows neither Idea nor Energy except through the Power that goes out from the Idea and Energy and returns to him. In the triune Godhead the Persons are both consubstantial and coequal. But such is not the case with the human artist, whose work is liable to be lopsided and "heretical," displaying an overemphasis on one of the Persons of the Trinity. The authors who are "Father-ridden" will try to "impose the Idea directly upon the mind and senses, believing that this is the whole of the work." The "Son-ridden poet will produce poems which will be sensuous or witty or flowery but lacking in coherence or a ruling idea.[33] The "Ghost-ridden" poet will strive for emotional effect without either coherence or attention to technique. But the more closely Idea, Energy, and Power are coequal in the writer (as in the Trinity), the better will be the work of literary art.[34]

CHAPTER FOUR

SACRAMENT, SYMBOL, AND MYTH

Sacramentalism and Criticism

The previous chapter has demonstrated the importance of the doctrine of
the Incarnation for Christian Criticism, especially in combatting the tendency to "angelism" and the consequent neglect of the particular. One of
the most vigorous exponents of such Incarnationalism is Malcolm Ross, who
makes an important connection between the Incarnation and Christian sacramentalism:

[T] he Incarnation makes possible, indeed demands, the sacramental vision of
reality. The flesh, the world, things, are restored to dignity because they are
made valid again. Existence becomes a drama which, no matter how painful
it may be, is nevertheless meaningful. And no detail in the drama is without its utterly unique reality. No thing is insignificant . . . the Christian artist, when he knows what he is about, respects the practical, objective limits
of form. He cannot be, as Shelley was, the poet of an "unbodied joy." Nor
may he seek to break through the illusion of sense experience into a realm
of pure essence or even into a realm of pure art-vision, that verbal universe
of the seer tricked out as a special kind of reality, sometimes even as the
only reality.

For Ross, Incarnation is necessary to "the whole life of Christian symbol
in all its reaches," and he goes on specifically to connect it with the Eucharist, "the rite whereby eternally the Word is made flesh." Like Lynch, Ross
sees the sense of the analogical "perpetuated" by the Eucharistic liturgy,

which applies the eternal sacrifice of Christ to man within time, and which does not scorn to use the concrete man-made elements of bread and wine in the redemptive process.[1]

However, to Ross the proper analogical validation of the concrete and the temporal is possible only, it would seem, within the context of the dogma of transubstantiation. He contends that the separation of nature from grace, of history or time from religion, followed upon the Protestant Reformation of the sixteenth century and has had a detrimental effect on poetry. He charges Luther with a "wholly individualistic and subjective" Eucharistic cult which retained only the rhetorical and ceremonial level of Catholic sacramentalism. Calvin went to the opposite extreme, stressing corporate worship rather than subjective experience but doing away with sacramentalism and reducing the sacramental symbols to "bare figures." Thus he separated divine power from time and from matter and paved the way for the total secularism which has swept over Western culture.[2]

The resulting dissociation of sensibility is encountered not only in Milton, in whose writing dogma is subjectivized and made to serve the private ideas of the poet. In the Anglican poets of the seventeenth century as well, dogma and rhetoric are separated: symbol declines into metaphor, poetry dissolves into "bloodless abstraction," and eventually into the "witty generalities" of Alexander Pope. In the last two centuries we have on the one hand the world, nature, which became the domain of science and naturalism; on the other hand there are "spirit" and "idea," which have become subjectivized and psychologized. Even Roman Catholicism became defensive and was unable until recently to affirm sacramentalism in the natural or social orders.[3] It is only in the past several decades, in such writers as Bernanos, Auden, and Eliot, that we see artists in the West struggling towards a true Christian sacramentalism in which time and the world are bearers of divine grace.

Ross writes shortly before the revived interest in sacramentalism and liturgy among Protestants, and before Vatican Council II inspired Roman Catholic theologians to a new "openness" to other Christians and to the world. It is this openness to the world that Amos N. Wilder, in refuting Ross, contends is more characteristic of Protestantism than traditional Roman Catholicism. "The Catholic insists on the concreteness of a supernatural order of sacrament and symbol, an objective and therefore essentially static world of mediating imagery. A Protestant understanding of grace and nature foregoes such an impressive fixed 'firmament of symbol,'

but it retains the advantages—with all the risks—of the immediate Word, free
to engage itself without trammels in all the actualities of the world."[4]

Very different in tone is "Art and Sacrament" by the Welsh painter and
poet David Jones, which, in its latinate scholasticism, is very Roman—though
it is not polemical and indeed is designated "An Enquiry." Jones takes two
lines of argument. The first is anthropological: man is by nature *homo
poeta,* whose making is not merely utilitarian; man *makes* out of his free
will, and his making has in it the elements of the gratuitous, the intransitive.
Man is also a sign-making animal: the things he makes are "the signs of
something other." This is the distinguishing mark of humanity; even paleo-
lithic man "juxtaposed marks on surfaces not with merely utile, but with
significant, intent; that is to say a 're-presenting,' a 'showing again under
other forms,' an 'effective recalling' of something was intended."[5]

The second line of argument is specifically Christian and serves to supplement the first, which could be called "natural."[6] Jones claims that another
word for "sign-making" is "sacramental": thus the observation that men
make signs could be rephrased *men make sacraments.* For the Christian this
characteristic is especially important, since Jesus himself, the perfect and
representative man, was a maker of signs. The Crucifixion itself involved
signs: "For what was accomplished on the Tree of the Cross presupposes
the sign-world and looks back to foreshadowing rites and arts of mediation
and conjugation stretching back for tens of thousands of years in actual pre-
history." Furthermore, on the day before he suffered, Jesus in the Upper
Room "did something and said something which no matter how it is theologically interpreted and no matter what its interrelatedness to what was
done on the Hill, was unmistakably and undeniably a sign-making and a rite-
making and so an act of Ars; moreover an act to be, in some sense, repeated." So it was understood among his followers, among whom certain
acts involving "the signs of the quasi-artifacts of bread and wine" were
mandatory. It is appropriate, then, to refer to Christ not only as "a man
along with us" but as "man-the-artist along with us," and "the Artifex, the
Son."[7] Despite the commitment of mankind to natural sacramentalism,
Jones wonders whether modern technocratic civilization is not alienating
man from his inherent habit of sign-making, so that men will reject even
dogmatic sacramentalism.

Until recently no critic outside the Roman Communion, so far as I know,
has attempted an extended sacramental theory of art as have Ross and
Jones, though Anglican critics have been conscious of the relationship in

practical criticism. Martin Jarrett-Kerr lauds Dostoyevsky for his "sacramental" view of nature. In an early book Nathan A. Scott, Jr., discussing the modern Italian writer Ignazio Silone, speaks of his "essentially liturgical conception of the problem of society." Those characters, he writes, "who devote themselves to [the] work of redemption, that was initiated by Christ, are in truth extensions of his Presence: in their action is contained a sacramental quality which we must apprehend and lay hold of, if we are to be saved from the wreckage and disorder of contemporary history." And Paul Elman states,"The Church has enshrined the necessity of concretion in its sacramental theology, recognizing for example in its eucharistic doctrine the banality of bread and wine transfigured by its explicit relation to the Ground of Being."[8] The sacramental orientation of these comments stems, no doubt, from the sacramental orientation of Anglican theology. The view of the Eucharist as an extension of the Incarnation is a strongly Anglican emphasis.

Only lately has Scott attempted to spell out a specifically sacramental poetic. He summarizes the argument of Erich Auerbach that Christianity replaced the Classical tendency to split the sublime from the realistic by the Christian belief that the ordinary, the common, the historical is open to divine significance. This is inherent in the notion of *figura:* events and personages, though chronologically removed from one another, could be analogically related, as for example Adam was a *figura* of Christ. The figural imagination operates, of course, in the Hebrew-Christian Scriptures and in medieval literature, most famously in *The Divine Comedy.* But Dante's portrayal of reality, Auerbach notes, is so vivid that it overshadows its spiritual significance—and from this point on the image of God became less and less important in comparison with the image of man, until the nineteenth-century emphasis on "fact" by such men as Flaubert and Zola produced, in turn, a revulsion from the outward world and a retreat to "inwardness" on the part of such writers as Valery and Joyce and Stevens.

During the past several decades, however, there has been a reaffirmation of what anthropologist Lucien Levy-Bruhl calls the "law of participation," a sense of human relatedness to "all the great realities, both animate and inanimate, into commerce with which he [man] is brought by the adventures of life."[9] This participation of man in the world, termed by Claude Levi-Strauss *la pensée sauvage,* has especially characterized modern nonrepresentational art, as well as the absurdist theatre and the more recent theatrical "happening," which does not separate audience from play as static object but involves the audience in a spontaneous and unfixed activity.

How is the Christian Critic, though, to counter the corrosiveness of technological positivism and recapture the figural connection between factuality and mystery? He can no longer, Scott judges, appeal to the traditional belief that the natural is the veil of the supernatural; nevertheless, it is possible to assert the sacramental principle of the "sacredness of the commonplace." Here Scott appeals to Heidegger's notion of *Gelassenheit,* or "meditative openness" to the claim that the world has on us. Only then can we contemplate Being, which is not an intellectual category but the mysterious source of reality which "hails" us and to which we respond by receptiveness to the plenitude of that which is not ourselves or of our making.[10] Heidegger recognized that the poet could respond more effectively than the philosopher to the presence of Being. Scott's example is Theodore Roethke, who, unlike many modern artists, does not feel it necessary to organize and create reality; instead, he is attentive to the music and mystery of things animate and inanimate.

But, almost as if to support Malcolm Ross's charge that Protestantism is nonsacramental, Protestant critics have attempted, to my knowledge, no theory of art or literature as sacramental. There are, however, some interesting remarks by the British nonconformist P.T. Forsyth. Instead of applying theological concepts to art, he applies the principles of Hegel's *Aesthetik* to religion. In this Forsyth is a man of the nineteenth century looking back to the days of German idealism, in which attempts were made to reconcile all the disparities of life in grand systems of philosophy. To Hegel Christianity was a synthesis of Greek naturalism and the Hebrew sense of God as transcendent: "If we marry penetrative Greek imagination to masterful Jewish spirituality, have we not that spiritual imagination which is the artistic feature of Christendom?"[11]

Also suggestive of the Hegelian attempt at synthesis are Forsyth's brief comments about the sacramentalism of art: "All art is sacramental in its nature. . . . The artist has a certain vision, which he embodies in a certain material form, with the object of conveying to poor me the same vision or the same mood. The outward is used by his inward to rouse a like inwardness in me. But his sacramental use of the outward is more than memorial, more than symbolic. He incarnates his vision, he does not merely suggest it. There is a certain transubstantiation."[12]

Symbol and Myth

In discussing the implications of sacramentalism for the Christian view of art, Christian Critics are alarmed at the tendency toward scientism and positivism. It is a commonplace, in fact, for commentators to observe that for the past three hundred years the range of what is regarded as meaningful discourse has been more and more delimited until uses of language which are not empirically verifiable—and this includes poetic and religious utterances —are viewed as meaningless. In response to this tendency, Malcolm Ross and David Jones maintain, each in his own way, that other levels—the symbolical and theological, for instance—are also in some sense "meaningful" and should not be ruled a priori out of bounds.

Others, too, are concerned with validating the symbolical and mythical levels of language. John McGill Krumm notices that there have been in recent years efforts to widen the scope of legitimate meaning: "The seventeenth-century assumption that all really important things can be discovered and known without recourse to what we should now call—without any derogatory implication—mythological truth is an assumption that would be widely challenged today by Christian theologians; also by poets, novelists, and dramatists; and by an influential school of modern philosophy which acknowledges the penetrating and illuminating power of symbols. The Biblical understanding of nature as sacramental in principle opens up a whole new dimension in nature which is never taken into account in scientific analysis and description."[13] Evidently, as Krumm intimates by speaking both of "mythological truth" and "the penetrating and illuminating power of symbols," the fate of symbol and myth are inextricably linked. Both are "sacramental," in David Jones's sense of the word; both "recollect" and "re-present" something other than themselves.

That myth or symbol is basic to the structure of literary art is the point made by Roy W. Battenhouse. Poetry is not to be judged as metaphysics or religion; the poet is a craftsman and is to be evaluated in terms of his skill as a maker with words. Nonetheless, a work of art "implies an order of metaphysical or religious valuation. The finished poem has an organization of symbol and a structure of myth which no merely esthetic reasons can account for." In an age when there are no commonly accepted interpretations of life, the search for mythic ordering of experience has become an acute problem for the artist. Christianity can, according to Battenhouse, furnish the poet "a completely adequate world of myth within which all things can be assigned their peculiar place in the total realm of experience and accorded their proportionate and proper value."[14]

Nathan A. Scott, Jr., in an essay on "Religious Symbolism in Contemporary Literature," uses an equally broad definition, speaking of the "radical technique of the imagination, whereby the poetic mind gives consent to a ruling myth that introduces order and coherence into the whole of that experience from which particular symbols spring and from which, in fact, they take their meaning." But whereas Battenhouse is interested in the relevance of Christianity to the poet, Scott's approach to literature is from the standpoint of the critic. Here, as we have seen him do before, he introduces theological concepts from Paul Tillich, asserting that "in turning to the writers of today who are presenting the most important testimony about the human condition, we may then regard the significant patterns of symbolism implicit in their work as religious in whatever degree to which they suggest the ultimate concerns of contemporary man." He then proceeds to pick out four mythic configurations that he sees to be important in modern literature: the myth of the Isolato (the term is from *Moby Dick*), the myth of Hell, the myth of Voyage, and the myth of Sanctity—and then he illustrates the four myths from various nineteenth- and twentieth-century writers such as Melville, Conrad, Joyce, Graham Greene, and Eliot.[15]

Another perspective on symbolism is offered by H.D. Lewis, who addresses himself to the problem of how we know God, for which he thinks neither rationalism nor mysticism, the traditional explanations, provides an adequate solution: rationalism leads only to formal knowledge, while mysticism involves "the absurdity of claiming to see things as God sees them, to have a transcendent experience." How then can we know God without falling into anthropomorphism? Lewis answers: "we have in art an awareness of reality in a form that is least reducible to the categories of our own thought, the world being thus presented in a way that has clearer traces of a sphere beyond that of finite experience itself." The artist is a seer; his function is to make people see beyond their ordinary perceptions, and he discloses new aspects of reality to which they had previously been blind. But he also encounters the incomprehensible: "in art there is an unveiling which is at the same time a concealment: in the very process of clarification there is also a deepening of mystery."[16] God is also both mystery and light, and the religious experience is a nonrational experience which imparts new insights into reality along with a sense of "otherness," of the unfathomable.

69

Furthermore, both artistic and religious experience are symbolic and are not translatable into rational abstractions as logic or mathematics is. Rational content is important for religion only "so far as it enters, together with the evaluation of its elements, into a whole of a very different nature in which it has no isolable function. . . .A transmutation occurs by which ideas, in a new medium and in combination with other factors, acquire a further recognisably religious import."[17] This closely parallels the dynamics of poetry, in which literal meaning is transmuted by the artistic medium, in combination with aesthetic factors, to acquire poetic meaning.

Finally, Lewis draws a further parallel between the "truth" of religion and the "truth" of art. Neither is true merely in the sense of abstract intellectual principles, but their truth is "given in events," in history, on the level of "arresting fact," of concrete particularity and experience. Thus both art and religion are symbolic of the "wholly other," a reality not ourselves. Both move us to "turn our minds out into the world, break out of the routine of our own orbit to voyage among things . . .; as the scriptures teach, we have to lose our own lives and then we may find that we have saved them."[18]

A similar argument is advanced by Ray Brett in "The Function of Literary Imagery in Christian Understanding." He notes that modern criticism holds that ambiguity, depth, and complexity are poetic virtues. Any translation of the poem into abstract terms is inadequate, for it does violence to the rich particularity of image and symbol in which poetic meaning is embodied. It is likewise futile to attempt to translate the Christian faith into a series of logical propositions, for the Holy Spirit works in terms of specific historical events; and the "meaning" of these events is more than any abstracted interpretation of them. This is notably true with the Scriptures themselves; as Brett remarks, "It is clear, as I see it, from modern New Testament criticism, that the Gospel story is not simply a naive *chronicling of historical events,* but a *theological interpretation of these events."* This is as true for the Epistles as for the Gospels: they are literary works, expressed in symbols and imagery whose patterns must be explored and explicated by the methods of literary criticism.[19]

The preoccupation of critics with myth and symbol has come under sharp attack from those who doubt its validity for the Christian. The first and major objection comes from those who hold that the Christian faith is essentially historical, whereas the kind of meaning that image and symbol involve is ahistorical; furthermore, there exists the danger of dehistoricizing

Christianity and reducing it to mere symbolic and mythic status.[20] Ronald
W. Hepburn contends that the disregarding of the problem of the historical
reliability is dangerous. It is true that the images are "untranslatable," but
it is also true that they "point beyond themselves into history." If we limit
ourselves only to an analysis of the images, we learn nothing about their his-
toricity.[21]

The second major class of objections to the preoccupation with myth and
symbol is philosophical; criticism has come from both the existentialist
camp and from the linguistic analysts. One of the most influential and con-
troversial schools of biblical theology in the twentieth century is that dominated by the Marburg New Testament scholar Rudolf Bultmann. It is his
contention that the world-view of the New Testament is mythological in that
it seeks to present the otherworldly and divine as appearing and acting on
the worldly and human level. But such prescientific discourse is no longer
viable for modern man. What then? Is the Bible to be thrown into the ash-
heap of primitive superstition? No. Concealed in the myth is the *kerygma,*
the divine word or proclamation addressed to man which must be "demyth-
ologized" to be relevant today. At this point Bultmann brings in the existential philosophy of Martin Heidegger: the New Testament is to be remythol-
ogized or restated as presenting the choice between unauthentic and authen-
tic existence, as offering freedom from anxiety and pride and a "new life" in
faith and love and obedience and openness to the future.[22]

Bultmann's proposals have been attacked repeatedly and on many
grounds, but perhaps most pertinent for our purposes is the criticism of
Roland M. Frye and Amos N. Wilder. Frye compares Bultmann to the biblicist Fundamentalists, who also deny the validity of the dramatic and symbolic in the Scriptures. But whereas Bultmann would reduce symbol and
myth to existentialist abstractions, the Fundamentalists insist on a literal
interpretation of the Bible stricter than that exercised by such Renaissance
Christians as Boccaccio and Sidney and Milton. Even the Protestant Re-
former John Calvin taught that the truth of God was "accommodated" to
finite and sometimes unscientific, unhistorical human conceptions. Wilder
opposes Bultmann on the basis of modern literary criticism, which has re-
minded us, he argues, that it is dangerous to attempt to reduce mytho-poetic
statement to abstract paraphrase. Such abstractions constitute a denigration
of myth that is unwarranted, for "mythological statement represents knowledge of a kind. It has a cognitive aspect. It represents not merely an emotional reaction to reality but a judgment about reality, an account of reality,

and an account based upon this kind of concrete and subtle experience."
Wilder is able to make this criticism because of his own high view of mythopoeic language; elsewhere he writes:

It is true that poetry, in the innumerable forms and genres that it takes on
in various cultures, has many roles that are largely unrelated to the religious
life. We must also recognize, as the Thomist would put it, that the artist
gives himself to the work in view where the believer presses on to communion with God. But such distinctions should not lead us to a denial of that
initial "epiphany" or world-making moment which lies behind all significant
poetry, particularly today when religious forms have lost much of their relevance for man's perennial need.[23]

There is also a growing group of theologians influenced by the positivist-
oriented linguistic analysis school; their attitude toward the meaning of
biblical and religious language is largely negative. They will not go so far as
did the early A.J. Ayer to deny all meaning to such discourse, but in seeking
to assert some kind of meaning for it they severely restrict its validity—for
instance, Paul Van Buren reduces the status of religious statement to an expression of one's private "blik," one's emotional attitude towards life which
is neither objectively verifiable nor subject to intellectual analysis.[24]

These theologians stress radical immanence; any belief in "spirit" or
"the transcendent," no matter how disguised in sophisticated metaphysics,
is a vestigial holdover from Platonic dualism and is no longer credible. Since
the etymology of the word symbol (from Greek *symballein:* to throw together) suggests an attempt to link two levels of reality, the possibility of
symbolic meaning is probably precluded as well.

If some theologians wish to collapse the transcendent into the immanent,
at least one writer, Nicolas Berdyaev, believes that the immanent-transcend-
ent dualism which gives rise to symbolism will ultimately give way to the
transcendent. It is true, he maintains, that all order, all meaning in the natural world is symbolic of the other, the spiritual world. The alternatives to
admitting this are to retire either into absolute psychologistic subjectivism
(as Kant did) or into naturalistic positivism, thus becoming enslaved to this
world. For "the symbolic conception of the world is the only profound one
and it alone manifests and makes clear the deep mysteries of being. The
whole of our natural life here below is devoid of meaning save when there
lies upon it a symbolic sanctity. . . ." By symbolic sanctity Berdyaev means
that in this world are perceived signs of another world which is infinite and

mysterious and spiritual. But he does not halt at a flesh-spirit dualism, the two levels connected only by symbol. In the Incarnation the Christian sees the entering of the infinite into the finite, the penetration of flesh by spirit. The coming of Christ into the world, in fact, proclaims the victory of spirit over flesh: "The obstinacy of the flesh is only the symbol of a fall in the spiritual world. But the illumination of the flesh manifested by the earthly life of the Son of God is the indication of a fresh uprising in the spiritual world."[25]

Art, too, looks to the ascendancy of spirit over flesh. The tragedy of art is that artistic creativity aims "to break out through 'this world' to another world, out of the chaotic, heavy and deformed world into the free and beautiful cosmos." But there is always a gap between aim and realization, for what happens is merely that artistic-cultural objects are created which are only symbols, shadows of the ideal world of true being. Classical art is satisfied with "culture": it is immanent, at home in this world. Christian-romantic art, in contrast, is not satisfied with formal perfection in this world, for "there is always a transcendental intention towards another world." But we are now at a critical transitional stage in history: both this-worldly art (whether it be called classicism or display the slavish subjection to this world of realism or naturalism) and romantic art are being surpassed by a "new symbolism" which is no longer satisfied with romantic longing. Even this symbolism is not the final achievement, though, according to Berdyaev. It in turn is making way for "theurgy," which is "art creating another world, another being, another life; creating beauty as essence, as being." What will characterize the new epoch of creativity is not the making of culture or art objects but a new working together of man with God which will be absolutely free from this world's limitations.[26]

CHAPTER FIVE

THE TRAGIC AND THE COMIC

The Tragic

Since the origin of drama is generally associated with religion—and drama indeed is seen by one writer to be of all the art forms the most closely related to the original art form, the holy dance[1]—it is not surprising that the dramatic forms, and the tragic and comic attitudes associated with them, have been highly significant to Christian Critics. Most scholars agree that during the two great periods of drama, in ancient Greece and in Renaissance Europe, what we have is the increasing artistic independence of drama from the *sacer ludus,* the holy play, which was originally liturgical in nature. But if Greek drama always remained religious (if not directly liturgical), drama in Europe and the English-speaking countries has, over the past six hundred years, been removed from proximity to the altar and has been thoroughly secularized.[2] There has also been in the Church perennial hostility to the stage, which has expressed itself, for instance, in the automatic excommunication of all actors, the closing of the London theatres by the Puritans in the seventeenth century, and the shunning of the theatre by some conservative Christians to this day.

This historic antipathy is still felt among Christian Critics. Indeed, one Roman Catholic critic, E.I. Watkin, goes so far as to say that there is "a necessary and essential incompatibility between drama and religion, a mutual exclusion of each by the other, which is grounded in their respective

natures."[3] Most Christian Critics, though, avoid such sweeping generalizations and direct their comments specifically to the relationship between
Christianity and the traditional modes of tragedy and comedy. Much of this
commentary, it must be admitted, is predominantly theoretical, so that
whatever contributions it makes to critical understanding are on the specu-
lative level: only occasionally do we get detailed analysis of a particular
work, but when this is done both the work and the theological-critical position of the critic are illumined. Often the theorist will focus on the similarity or dissimilarity between the tragic or comic *mythos* or plot and the
Christian *mythos* or story (usually patterned on the life, death, and resurrection of Christ). Or he may compare the Christian view of man with the
nature of the tragic or comic protagonist.

The problem of tragedy has attracted the most critical attention. Ironically, it seems that the first major critic who proclaimed that religion and
tragedy were at odds, I.A. Richards, was not himself a religionist but was
concerned with protecting what he felt to be an antireligious experience
from the eroding effect of religion. To obtain the tragic experience, the
psychological balance which derives from the catharsis of pity and terror,
Richards writes, "the mind does not shy away from anything, it does not
protect itself with any illusion, it stands uncomforted, unintimidated, alone
and self-reliant." It follows then that tragedy "is only possible to a mind
which is for the moment agnostic or Manichean. The least touch of any
theology which has a compensating Heaven to offer the tragic hero is
fatal."[4]

From a historical and philosophical perspective rather than a psychological one, the German philosopher Karl Jaspers concludes much the same
thing. The tragic sense, according to Jaspers, dissolves the rationalizations
of philosophy and the assurances of religion. No version of the accepted
myths can remain stable for the tragedian, and each playwright revises them
in his "passionate struggle for truth." This struggle means that tragedy will
ask ultimate questions, in visual and dramatic ways: "Why are things the
way they are? What is man? What leads him on? What is guilt? What is
fate? What are the ordinations valid among men, and where do they come
from? What are the gods?"[5]

Nonetheless these questions later become rationalized into philosophy,
Jaspers says, and instead of passionate questions there are constructed systems of thought which purport to establish universal harmony: the result
is that the tragic man is "liberated" into apathy. The other "liberation"

from tragedy is provided by revealed religion's offer of salvation. The discrepancies of life which are felt by tragedy are explained by Judaism and Christianity as the result of original sin, which enmeshes every man in guilt. But Christ is presented to the Christian as the redeemer who by choice identifies himself with sin and guilt to deliver man from them. Jaspers declares: "The chance of being saved destroys the tragic sense of being trapped without chance of escape. Therefore no genuinely Christian tragedy can exist."[6]

Richard Sewall, who also emphasizes that tragedy deals with human questioning in the face of an inexplicable universe, agrees essentially with Jaspers but does allow that Christianity brought with it a new self-consciousness. Sewall points out that neither the Greeks nor the Old Testament (not even Job) was greatly concerned with the examination of the soul or the inner life. The Christian, however, examined the soul and found therein utter guilt and condemnation which far surpassed the self-reproach of an Oedipus, who remained proud even in his downfall. And the Christian man, sinful though he was, now was faced with the agonizing dilemma of choosing blessedness or damnation. The new sensitivity that was his as a result of self-examination was not canceled out even when he believed in the salvation that was divinely proffered, Sewall maintains, for he had continually to examine his soul to ascertain whether indeed it remained in a state of grace. Therefore the terrifying possibilities of heaven and hell, of hope and despair, became a permanent part of Western man's experience.

Now it is true that during the Middle Ages the Mass took the place that the theatre doubtless had for the faithful at the ancient Dionysian festivals; for the Mass, like the ancient tragedies, portrayed suffering and sacrifice, and even provided a kind of cathartic effect. But there grew up in the late Middle Ages a new interest in evil, death, and damnation which began to cancel out the assurances of the Church and paved the way for the burst of tragedy in the sixteenth century. Those tragedies reflected the "inwardness" of Christian piety but directed it towards an expression of insecurity and despair.[7] The "inwardness" of Christian piety is as much as one can concede to Christianity, I suspect, if one views tragedy as essentially nihilistic. But such a position reveals as much about the antireligious bias of the theorists who hold it as it does about the nature of tragedy itself.

Most of the critics, however, who hold that tragedy and Christianity are incompatible are concerned not to preserve a notion of tragedy but to preserve Christianity. An early statement of this kind, one which has influenced subsequent criticism, is that of the Neo-Orthodox theologian Reinhold Niebuhr. In contrasting tragedy and Christianity he first sets up a definition of "true tragedy," which he distinguishes from most so-called tragedy, which is merely pitiful and pathetic. The novels of Hardy, for instance, are full of creatures who are pitiful dupes of inscrutable fate; and the plays of Ibsen have protagonists who are victims of self and immoral social conventions. True tragedy, in contrast, elicits reverence as well as pity, for a tragic hero defies a hostile universe in the assertion of his own soul's integrity; thus, according to Niebuhr, he suffers not because he is weak and pitiful but because he is strong, and he is pronounced guilty not on account of vice but on account of virtue. Furthermore, the hero inflicts suffering on himself, initiating it by a creative act against God, like Prometheus, or against the received morality, like Agamemnon or Orestes.[8]

With Christianity the situation is far different. First of all, the death which usually closes the tragic story does not close the Christian story, in which death is swallowed up in victory. The model here, of course, is Christ himself, whose crucifixion was the "resolution of tragedy. Here suffering is carried into the very life of God and overcome. It becomes the basis of salvation." The view of guilt is also different. Like classical tragedy, Christianity believes that guilt and creativity are interwoven; but whereas to the Greek tragedian creativity inevitably brings on guilt, to the Christian sin emerges not only out of creativity itself but out of human freedom, and is brought on by man's self-centeredness and egotism. Therefore the sinner, unlike the tragic hero, is not to be reverenced but only to be pitied. And sin is not to be seen as an ineluctable element in the universe. Paradoxically, the proof of this is the Cross itself. The crucified victim is sinless, but this very sinlessness on the part of the "Second Adam," the new representative of all humanity, indicates the essential goodness of man. The crucifixion also reveals that God is good (in contrast to the malevolent God whom the tragic hero defies) and that he overcomes evil with goodness.[9]

David Daiches Raphael comes at tragedy from a slightly different angle, though some of his arguments resemble those of Niebuhr. He cites two reasons why the biblical tradition is inimical to tragedy. First, both Judaism and Christianity believe that God is just, and therefore there must be an answer to the question, why do the innocent suffer? Christianity emphasizes the ultimate moral order of the world and speaks of original sin and the last judgment, whereas tragedy merely presents the struggle of man with incomprehensible evil and suffering and offers no solution to it. A second distinction between religion and tragedy is found in their respective notions of what constitutes the admirable man. In tragedy, Raphael explains, the hero defies nature, fate, the God which opposes him; and his defiance is more sublime than the power he defies. In Christianity nature and fate are governed by a just God, and defiance against God is blasphemous: what is admirable is humility and patience before the Almighty. Thus the Suffering Servant in Isaiah accepts suffering, Job is submissive to God, Milton's Samson and Corneille's Polyeucte choose death in order to execute God's justice. In this light, says Raphael, it is seen that Racine's "Christian" tragedies are not both Christian and tragic: his Athalie is not admirable in her defiance of God, whereas his Phèdre is tragically admirable and the Jansenistic God who decrees her damnation is vindictive. Shakespeare's *Lear* is often called a Christian tragedy, but Cordelia's fate is, to use A. C. Bradley's term, a "waste of goodness," and Lear, rather than bearing his fate, rages against the gods.[10]

A complex argument against the possibility of Christian tragedy is put forward by Edmond LaB. Cherbonnier. About the only attitude tragedy and Christianity have in common, he claims, is an antipathy towards the easy, sentimental optimism which held sway during the latter part of the nineteenth century. Otherwise, they are based on disparate ways of looking at the world. Tragedy relies on a "double vision" on the ultimate level: all the antinomies, opposites, and contradictions which appear in life—vitality and form, mind and matter, light and dark, etc.—are united. Hegel once wrote that "the Truth is in the whole." From this, Cherbonnier continues, one can infer that "an adequate philosophy of life must not only include everything, but must also *affirm* everything."[11] Thus the contraries of good and evil, positive and negative, are neutral and equally valid: to choose one above the other is to be partial and partisan. On the experiential level, however, man feels what he calls moral forces to be clashing and incompatible; and so the tragic hero finds himself choosing what he regards as one good at the expense of another good. Human freedom is thus seen as a matter of agonizing choice, and inevitably involves man in moral dilemmas and condemnation because of his partiality.

Summing up, Cherbonnier writes that the "philosophical stage setting" for tragedy includes "two shifting backdrops: the *ultimate perspective* of the detached observer, of the aesthete, in which all differences cancel each other out and in which no discord is possible; and the *finite perspective* of the man of action, in which strife and contradiction are the rule." This double perspective accounts for the hubris of the tragic hero, which can take two forms: "Either the hero treats some segment of reality as though it were the whole (in philosophical terms, he 'absolutizes the relative'), and thus calls down upon himself the vengeance of ultimate reality; or he strives consciously to introduce absolute perfection into this merely relative world which, by definition, cannot stand perfection, and thus he inexorably exacts the death penalty." As heroes of the first type Cherbonnier includes Hamlet, who absolutizes the desire for redress of injustice; Antigone, who absolutizes family loyalty; and Lady Macbeth, who absolutizes emotional honesty. The prototype of the second sort of hero is Prometheus, who tries to introduce the arts of heaven into the imperfect world of man.[12]

This double perspective is also enjoined on the spectator of tragedy, who must hold both views in tension; if the tension is relaxed, the tragic effect is destroyed. If the spectator focuses on the finite, he sees not tragedy but a morality play, in which goodness must be depicted as triumphant and evil punished, or he sees only "unrelieved frustration." If he focuses on the ultimate, he sees not tragedy but comedy. But if he succeeds in maintaining the precarious doubleness between the finite and infinite, he will be rewarded with a kind of spiritual catharsis, for he will realize (from his vantage point outside the play), even as he sees the hero in his finitude devise his own doom, that "everything happens in accord with a universal law of compensation, that the hero's suffering is really only the necessary restoration of the metaphysical balance."[13]

The biblical philosophy, according to Cherbonnier, denies the double perspective integral to tragedy. The Bible offers only one view, one perspective, because God is Creator of both heaven and earth. Therefore the Greek distinction between infinite and finite is not valid, as the infinite God himself proved by becoming finite "Flesh." Neither is it hubris to apply earthly ideas to the divine, for "the same words which apply peculiarly to human beings, as distinct from the rest of creation, are the very words which provide the clue to the nature of God: will, purpose, responsibility, intelligence, the discrimination of good and evil, forgiveness, love, even chagrin."[14] There is, it is true, a "discrepancy" between human life and the will of God; however, this discrepancy is not essential to the structure of being but, rather, contingent on man's moral choices. These moral choices are not between opposites that are neutral but between good and evil, forces that will not ultimately be merged in some final metaphysical unity. Moral partisanship is thus the appropriate response to the world rather than the cause of human downfall.

The role of the observer of biblical drama is also at odds with the role of the observer of tragedy, who is above the dramatic conflict because of his "ultimate" perspective. Since there is no separable infinite perspective in the biblical view, the observer is subject to the same clashes and conflicts as the dramatic character, and must be himself an active moral participant in the drama; in this way "he becomes vulnerable to the very emotion which tragedy would purge away."[15] He is able to weep at human suffering, but is able also to feel joy and hope because the love of God has been made available on the level of experiential human reality.

Cherbonnier's argument that the tragic perspective is dissolved if the spectator takes the "ultimate" point of view seems precisely the objection of E.I. Watkin to tragedy. He charges that the observer of tragedy must accept the perception of life's conflicts and experiences that characterizes the natural or unregenerate man. But the Christian, Watkin claims, cannot be satisfied with this perception, for religion "lifts us to a height from which we can look down upon the conflict of these [human] values, therefore upon the tragic conflict, as a battle for shadows." Thus, for example, Romeo's passion, Othello's jealousy, Shylock's revenge, and Hedda Gabler's ambition are not lasting. Only salvation and damnation matter, as in the case of Desdemona and Iago, respectively. The traditional account of Christ's life provides the pattern for this viewpoint, for it "presents an inevitable and foreknown triumph of the Divine Reality" and is therefore not drama, for it has, finally, no dramatic conflict or tragic failure.[16] Watkin does admit that drama cannot be as easily dispensed with as his argument might imply, but he allows a very inferior place for it: men participate in tragedy only insofar as their religious vision is inconsistent.

A midpoint between the positions of Watkin and Cherbonnier is taken by Laurence Michel, who differentiates between the tragic possibilities under the Old Testament dispensation and the preclusion of tragedy under the New Covenant of Christ. In the Old Testament there are present the two necessary conditions of tragedy: the inscrutability of God in the background, and in the foreground human evil. Were there not the first element, "the story would lose its power, and degenerate into a kind of ethicism." Without the second, "the story escapes from the human realm, and becomes an abstract intellectual speculation." Man is free to choose evil and suffer the consequences, but if he is obedient he may speak to God and be chosen to speak for him. All this, however, involves man acting and deciding in time and in the world, individually, and therefore he remains responding and questioning.[17] Even Job, though he finally submits, obtains no final answers.

The New Covenant is radically different, for in Christ man is given the hope of an already-obtained entrance into eternal joy. In addition, the sacraments are God coming and staying with man. In the New Dispensation, then, tragedy is no longer possible, except for those who, like the Manicheans, Calvinists, and Jansenists, insist on a basically Old Testament rather than New Testament view. Thus Racine's religious tragedies grow out of his Jansenist training. Dostoyevsky's *Crime and Punishment* and *The Brothers Karamazov* show the influence of the Book of Job, which he read at the age of eight and never forgot, as well as the influence of a Russian Orthodoxy whose Christ is strangely different from the Christ of the West. The American Puritan tragedians, too—Hawthorne, Melville, and Faulkner—and the contemporary "radical gropers"—Greene, Mauriac, Bloy, and Bernanos—possess an essentially Old Testament or Manichean vision: there is the devil effecting ruin in the world, but there is no saving power, no eschatological hope in the world.

A similar distinction between the Old and New Covenants is made by J.A. Bryant, Jr. Like Michel, Bryant recognizes that the full Christian story encompasses both the fall of the first Adam and the restoration of man in the Second Adam, Christ; thus it is (as Dante perceived) comic, not tragic. But is tragedy precluded? The Christian admits that the fall of Adam in Genesis is tragic, for we have the discrepancy between the undistorted image of God in man and the distortion of the image caused by Adam's freely willed disobedience. In the Christian Dispensation it is still true that man can disobey God and "fall." Bryant points out that the fall of the Christian is, in fact, "far more tragic than Adam's, for as a result of the incarnation of God in Jesus he can see more clearly the image of the creator in his own flesh and in his own actions." Christian tragedy is therefore possible in that it "discovers what remains of the divine image in man and contrasts the original perfection of that image with man's present fallen state." As well as revealing his present weakness and pride, however, it may show man coming to a humble knowledge of his dependence on supernatural grace.[18]

Bryant works out this theory in terms of the tragedies of Shakespeare. For instance, Hamlet's tragic fault is the desire for personal revenge, which causes him to disobey the Ghost's commission that he kill without hatred as God's minister of justice against Claudius. It is only in the last two acts that he comes to realize his sinfulness and his common fallibility with all men. Othello's fault is that he allows Iago to goad him into usurping the prerogative of God and acting as judge and executioner to Desdemona: thus the Moor, who begins the play described in almost divine terms, at the end must admit that his life has been a "vain boast."[19] Macbeth's fault is that he pre-empts the rule of God's providence and tries to fulfill the witches' prophecies himself. This, Bryant points out with evidence from Elizabethan homilies and sermons, is no less than apostasy, revolt against God, which is utterly damning because the apostate refuses to repent. Bryant also labels *Antony and Cleopatra* a tragedy, though his portrait of Antony as a paragon of manly virtues seems to outshine his description of Antony's loss of his "worthiest self" for the extravagant love of Cleopatra. On her part, Cleopatra is transformed by the death of Antony into a woman ready to die with dignity rather than submit to an insensitive Caesar.

Roy W. Battenhouse, very likely the most prominent theological critic of Shakespeare, quotes an earlier essay by Bryant in which Bryant "places" the various genres in relation to the Christian story of death in the Old Adam and new life through the New Adam, Christ; each genre represents one fragment of the whole. Battenhouse builds on this idea and theorizes that tragedy is analogous to the fall and death of the Old Adam, though his reading of specific tragedies is often different from that of Bryant.[20] Thus the tragic heroism which the romantics and modernists hail as admirable constitutes a parody of Christ's sacrificial heroism. Hamlet, for example, is sometimes viewed as undergoing a Christ-like suffering in obedience to the will of his father. But Battenhouse disagrees: "Whereas God in Christ put on flesh, that is humanity, in order that through this Man the world might be saved, Hamlet (substituting a reverse kind of incarnation) relinquishes his humanity to put on a mask of madness and thus visit a wicked world with his condemnation. Biblical echoes are here, but all of them in a transvalued version, a counterfeit version, an unwitting parody of atonement." A similar interpretation is put on other plays. The death of Lucrece in the *Rape of Lucrece* is a "staged suicide . . . paganism's dark substitute for the Christian Passion story." And at the end of *Antony and Cleopatra* "Antony . . . becomes an ironic Christ. His side pierced, he is lifted up limp on a stone monument, to commit there his spirit to Cleopatra's arms. . . . Within Egypt's pyramid she then stages a self-immolation which unwittingly parodies a crucifixion."[21]

To further elaborate the parodic nature of Christian tragedy, Battenhouse turns to Aristotle's discussion of *hamartia, anagnorisis,* and *catharsis,* and to Christian theology, especially that of Augustine and Aquinas. In the *Poetics* hamartia is basically intellectual; it involves error of judgment due to immoderation, and insofar as judgment (choice) is exercised on the basis of rationality hampered by passion or ignorance, the evil act is more or less pardonable. Thus Antigone immoderately insists on honor to the gods, and Oedipus acts not knowing who he is, regretting his action when he is apprised of the full circumstances. For the Christian commentators, however, more than intellect is involved: man's inclinations are perverted by original sin so that he chooses the evil, the distorted or partial, over the good or the complete. The human soul pridefully abandons love of God and embraces self-love, becoming a kind of end to itself and growing ignorant, weak, malicious, and concupiscent. Hamlet is discussed most fully as the exemplar of this self-love: he follows the directions of a fiend from hell, and his subsequent violent acts stem from his being spiritually drunk with "vainglorious imaginations" which fill his mind with incestuous and homosexual desires, narcissism, and irrationality. The same vaingloriousness motivates Lear to accept the flattery of his daughters, and this flaw leads to his downfall. Love of praise and glory also moves Coriolanus to scorn the people, and to accede to his mother's pleas for Rome and forget his responsibility to the Volscians with whom he has sided.[22]

The Aristotelian term *anagnorisis,* self-discovery, has often been interpreted as leading to regeneration for the tragic protagonist. But such, argues Battenhouse, is not the case with Shakespeare's tragedies, in which this recognition merely leads to "a despairing self-abandonment" to violence. At the graveyard Hamlet realizes he is doomed: now he becomes passive, letting the king act against him until the play ends and the stage is strewn with bodies. Richard II recognizes, toward the end, that he is faced with death; he seizes a weapon from one of his murderers, kills two men, despairs, and dies. Battenhouse also notes that Antony and Cleopatra are caught in a net of idolatrous and destructive *eros;* after they flee from Actium and are disgraced, they realize that their fortunes have turned—but this knowledge does not issue in repentance.[23]

Regarding the much-disputed notion of *catharsis,* Battenhouse accepts, and modifies, the explanation of S.H. Butcher that catharsis is "a clarification of the passions through the throwing off of some morbid element in them." Catharsis is indirectly moral, therefore, because it does away with certain obstacles to virtue; in other words, he continues, "a tragedy offers us opportunity for a learning to pity and fear what we ought to pity and to fear. Its function is the education of our emotions." He then applies this interpretation to several plays, including *Richard II* and *Hamlet,* but perhaps most succinctly to *Macbeth.* Shakespeare, it would appear, takes great pains to present Macbeth as one whose villainies, paradoxically, spring from an intention to be courageous, and whose conscience is deeply divided as he begins to involve himself in murder and withchcraft. In his vacillation and increasing despair we, the audience, experience deepening pity and fear because we can imagine ourselves acting as waveringly and as culpably—even as Macbeth, in growing awareness of the immoral nature of his actions, comes to understand the ambiguity of the witches' promise, the consequences of Lady Macbeth's urgings, and, perhaps most powerfully, the loss of "heaven's blessings on one's everyday existence."[24]

Many of the arguments that critics use against the possibility of Christian tragedy are also used to argue for such a possibility. I would judge that the man who probably began the modern defense of Christian tragedy, in the 1930s (and thus prompted some of the negative criticism surveyed above), was G. Wilson Knight, whose criticism along with that of his disciples has been dubbed "The School of Knight."[25] In an often-quoted theoretical justification of his approach to tragedy, Knight compares tragedy to the Mass, citing the anthropologists' view that both grew out of pagan sacrificial rituals: "The king was important in pagan ritual; his life, the life of the community; his death, their death; his renewal, their redemption and resurrection. In paganism too we have the dying and resurrected god. In Christianity we find these themes blended, with a king not of temporal but of spiritual power and authority and one whose sacrifice is a consciously willed act wherein ritual and ethic become one." The theory covers not only the individual tragic play but the overall pattern of Shakespeare's work, for he continues: "Shakespeare's final plays celebrate the victory and the glory, the resurrection and the renewal, that in the Christian story and in its reflection in Christian ritual succeed the sacrifice."[26]

We have seen that the major objection to Christian tragedy has been that the final victory of Christ transcends the tragic dilemma and defeat. Some critics, like Reinhold Niebuhr, feel that this precludes tragedy altogether; others, like Battenhouse, hold that tragedy is a permissible part of the Christian story but not all of it. Knight looks at the structure of tragedy as displaying the entire Christian story, including the final victory; thus the tragic hero is seen as a "miniature Christ" undergoing a calvary and a subsequent ascent. Accordingly, Othello, in the last scene, is victorious rather than defeated by Iago: "His ravings are not final: he rises beyond them. He slays Desdemona finally not so much in rage, as for 'the cause' (V.ii.346). He

slays her in love." *Lear* is a tragedy close to comedy; at the end there
emerges "a religion born of disillusionment, suffering, and sympathy." So
at the end the good forces, not the evil, win. And Timon of Athens becomes
at the last Christ-like, suffering for the pains of all men and finding a paradise above the world.[27]

The major weakness of Knight's stress on the triumph and optimism of
tragedy is that it blurs the distinction between tragedy and tragicomedy or
comedy. Many other Christian Critics, who along with Knight would argue
that Christianity and tragedy are compatible, avoid this weakness, placing
more emphasis on the negative side of the tragic experience while at the
same time denying that this negativity severs tragedy from Christianity.
Against those who claim that Christianity offers release and compensation
from death and suffering (and thus transcends tragedy), A.F. Glencross
argues that the Christian faith does not do away with suffering and death.
Shakespeare's Macbeth cries out against death, feeling that it is really evil.
Cleopatra at the end scorns the mundane world, but feels, like Macbeth, that
death involves a real physical loss without any compensatory reward for life.
Even the individual Christian does not have God's perspective, and experiences suffering and death as humanly real enough: Christ himself experienced them. And it is out of such human experience that tragedy is
written.[28]

A somewhat similar perspective is held by David E. Roberts, who takes
to task those critics who claim that classic tragedy rests in the fact that life
is full of perplexities and injustices, whereas Christianity escapes from the
tragic dilemma. Roberts proceeds to argue that the Greek tragedians were
not satisfied with a mere iteration of the unsolvable inequities of the human
condition; instead, they attempted to show the interaction between men
and the gods, the human and divine wills. In Aeschylus, it is true, the audience was to see the vengefulness of Zeus in *Prometheus Bound;* but it was
also to see that Prometheus was a rebel against heaven. In the *Oresteia* the
audience was to see that Antigone and Orestes were pursued by the Furies
in the very act of remaining faithful to sacred duty. There is mystery here
—mystery at the point where human resources fail and any resolution of the
dilemma "lies in an everlasting mercy for which men can do little more than
hope."[29] In the tragedies of Sophocles human character and motivation are
more important, but here, too, we see human suffering (as in the case of
Oedipus) which cannot be equated with human sin; but this causes Sophocles to look through the riddle of human existence to the divine harmony

beyond, to go beyond desperation to reconciliation, as Oedipus did upon finding that he was the object of his own curse, and as the entire play *Oedipus at Colonus* demonstrates. In Euripides the orthodox religious answers are no longer considered adequate; but even here we have a kind of appeal through the human predicament to the insistence that if there is a divine will, it must be morally good, it must ratify human reason and human compassion rather than violate them. There is also (and here Euripides is a "modern") a search for an "aesthetic" faith as an alternative to religious faith: since religious certitude is impossible and comfort derived from faith therefore unsure, let poetry refine beauty from suffering.

In none of the Athenian dramatists—not even in Euripides—is there the kind of nihilism that some contemporary theorists of tragedy insist upon, who call for the necessity of courageous despair in the face of an irremediable human plight. All three of the great tragedians would hold that there is no neat theological or philosophical system that accounts for the complex and sometimes inexplicable interweaving of fate and responsibility, despair and faith, and that any peace or salvation is to be reached not by sudden leaps of faith into empyrean serenity but by passing through the "fiery whirlwind" of human ambiguities. Roberts thus posits a dualism between the human and divine perspectives which is somewhat like that of the Protestant Neo-Calvinist theologians, though it is not as absolute as that advanced by Glencross, since one may apprehend experience redemptively and thereby transcend it. This ameliorated dualism is not, as some would have it, disconsonant with the Christian faith; and here Roberts points to the experience of Christ as his authority: "at the center of the gospel is the fact that God himself stands beyond tragedy only by passing through it with us."[30]

This "passing through" full human despair is the characteristic dimension of tragedy, according to William Lynch. Accordingly, we see in the great tragedies a line of dramatic movement from great energy in the first acts to a point towards the end where all energy is depleted, and the human will broken. With Oedipus we begin with a confident king speaking in full iambs, and at the close we have a poor, ruined, stuttering man who is unable to complete the last poetic foot. So with Shakespeare's protagonists: Macbeth, for instance, as a result of the witches' prophecies considers himself invincible, but eventually is reduced to thinking life idiotic and meaningless. Lynch observes that the region of the tragic is "a place where the human spirit 'dies' in frequent real helplessness," where human will and strength are seen to be inadequate. It is also what the theologian calls the place of faith, for only upon "dying" will the human mind "rise to a higher knowledge and insight."[31]

Christianity, as we have noted, is often blamed for blunting the tragic dilemma and making for comedy and romance. Lynch argues that it is rather the modern attempts at tragedy which actually bypass tragedy by asserting a romantically humanistic triumph on the part of the hero. Playwrights like Ibsen, Maxwell Anderson, and Eugene O'Neill refuse to allow their heroes the necessary descent into despair, and in the final acts of their plays they tack on some improbable angelic leap into the infinite. Their heroes nave not earned the dignity and courage and transcendence ascribed to them at the last.[32]

An exposition of tragedy which incorporates the theory of Lynch and also takes into account the work of Francis Fergusson and Murray Krieger is offered by Nathan A. Scott, Jr. The essential myth or fable which shapes tragedy, Scott observes, describes a schism, a split between existential experience of futility and meaninglessness, and the idea of good or justice in the world. So for Job, Oedipus, and Ahab we have the feeling that the universe is unjust and wasteful. The result for the tragic hero is moral "nausea and vertigo" at the collapse of the world's order. He is seized with anxiety and dread, which drive him to seek alleviation and release by a radical and defiant self-assertion. But such assertion, whether it be in terms of enlightenment, as with Prometheus, or punishment of regicide, as with Oedipus, or the encounter with cosmic malignity, as with Ahab, is inevitably partial because the tragic protagonist's vision is necessarily incomplete and finite: therefore, in his attempt to transcend his agony he makes wrong decisions and brings guilt on himself, and consequent suffering as punishment. Hubris, then, is not properly seen as egotistical pride per se but the "presumptuousness" of the protagonist in daring to assert himself.

Here Scott draws on Francis Fergusson's schema of Purpose, Passion, and Perception. The Purpose is the defiance of the protagonist; the Passion is the agony into which he is thrown because his assertion cannot overpower the facts of his experience; the Perception is the final disenchantment that human life is defeated and doomed. Thus to Fergusson as well as to many other recent theoreticians of tragedy, some of whom have been dealt with above, the tragic vision is "an unpalliated vision of shock and crisis, and of man in the extremest possible situation where all guarantees of meaning and security in his pilgrimage on earth have disappeared," a view which clashes with the notion that tragedy issues in a cathartic reconciliation between man and the universe. How then, asks Scott, are we to choose between the two views? He does not choose between them; he accepts them both, with the help of Murray Krieger's distinction between the ultimate absurdity of the tragic vision as experienced, say, by the hero of Kafka's *The Trial,* and the more affirmative view of tragic form: "Even when the final scene on the tragedian's stage is a scene of wreckage, woe, and utter defeat, the disaster and the doom are not altogether unbearable. For the very fact that tragedy is an aesthetic form means that what is substantive—the tragic vision—has been shaped, has been contained."[33]

In this way Scott is able to offer an answer in the debate over the possibility of Christian tragedy. Since the very aesthetic form of tragedy "must in some measure conciliate or resolve the dissonances of the tragic vision, it will achieve this transcendence only by invoking some principle of healing and redemption" and is consonant with the Christian principle of redemption. But the tragic vision, as distinct from the tragic form, is not so easily harmonized with Christianity, as theorists like Karl Jaspers have recognized. However, the position of critics like Jaspers does not take into account several aspects of Christian theology. First, Jaspers ignores "the vibrant eschatological tension that is so much a part of the Gospel."[34] Though Christ has come and "the End" has arrived, man's life is still marked by sin and suffering, and the Church waits the final fulfillment of the Gospel promise; in this sense the End is not yet.

What, though, is to be said to those Christians who hold a "realized" eschatology—the position that the "End" has "already entered the historical process in Jesus Christ"? Here Scott appeals to the prototype of Christ, whose life does not exhibit a lordship of power and glory but of humility and suffering and service, in which the Christian must join. This is the pattern not only of Christ's life but also of the Eucharist, in which the believer participates here and now, offering up his own life in conjunction with the sacrifice of Christ.[35] Man is not magically carried off to some heavenly sphere and released from the responsibility of this world; he receives grace to live in this world, through which he must pass before he can glimpse any other. Thus, though the Christian cannot accept an unmitigated tragic vision, he does experience human suffering; therefore Christianity and tragedy are not absolutely antithetical.

A more biblical approach is that of E.J. Tinsley, who takes issue with the position exemplified by Laurence Michel that Old Testament religion is tragic but that New Testament religion is not. Tinsley does recognize "tragic elements" in the Old Testament, which include the lack in most of the Old Testament of a belief in life after death, as well as "a nervous insecurity about the adequacy and finality of atonement. Sacrificial atonement availed only for those within the Covenant of Israel and even there for sins not done 'with a high hand.'" But these elements are eventually overcome by a faith which can "leap through tragedy." This leap was made possible by two strains in Hebrew religion: (1) "the belief that the universe is created and therefore redeemable" and (2) "the eschatology of a religion of promise and the hope which this caused to be born again and again." Tinsley does agree with Michel that the New Testament is "beyond tragedy," yet this does not mean that the tragic dimension is removed from the Christian life. He quotes Saint Paul, who refers to the Christian life as a "dying and rising" with Christ; this typifies the New Testament attitude that "belief does take a man through and beyond the tragic, but compassion involves a re-entry into the tragic experience."[36]

Tinsley then examines the theological climate for clues as to why Christianity and tragedy have been thought antithetical. He first castigates classical theology as being too Hellenic in its emphasis on divine impassibility, the idea that God, and therefore also Christ in his divine nature, are incapable of suffering. It has been only in recent decades that theological emphasis has been placed on the complete participation of Christ in human tragic experience. A second factor in Christian thinking about tragedy has been the recent drift towards Pelagianism, the idea that man is morally perfectible and does not need atonement. The idea of original sin, "which sees man as both victim and culprit," is necessary to the tragic view but has been unpopular in modern times. Thirdly, says Tinsley, the tendency to universalism, the belief that all men will eventually be saved, has made the tragic view unpalatable.[37]

It has probably been evident that many of the critics who defend the possibility of a Christian tragedy have regarded ancient Greek tragedy as the model of the genre. Let us now look at two theorists who are interested in pointing out the differences between Greek and Christian tragedy. One is W.H. Auden, who draws distinctions regarding (1) freedom of the will and (2) the nature of tragic hubris. On freedom he writes: "Greek tragedy is the tragedy of necessity; i.e., the feeling aroused in the spectator is 'What a pity it had to be this way'; Christian tragedy is the tragedy of possibility, 'What a pity it was this way when it might have been otherwise.'" Hubris

in Greek tragedy is "the illusion of a man who knows himself strong and believes that nothing can shake that strength, while the corresponding Christian sin of Pride is the illusion of a man who knows himself weak but believes he can by his own efforts transcend that weakness and become
strong." The Greek tragic hero begins in *arete* but plunges into exceptional
suffering: "He suffers because he has come into collision, not with other
individuals, but with the universal law of righteousness. As a rule, however,
the actual violation of which he is guilty is not his own conscious choice in
the sense that he could have avoided it. The typical Greek tragic situation
is one in which whatever the hero does must be wrong." It is wrong because
he is guilty of an overweening self-confidence with which he believes he is a
god who cannot suffer.[38] This is, moreover, the necessary condition of the
hero: if one is a hero he must therefore be guilty of hubris and be punished
by the gods. The suffering which results is an expiation for his sin, though
it is solely up to the gods to decide when his expiation is sufficient.

The fate of the Christian tragic hero, in contrast, is one of choice, as
Auden illustrates by way of Melville's Captain Ahab. At the beginning of
Moby Dick Ahab is what the Greek hero, such as Oedipus, is at the end:
exceptionally unfortunate. In the Greek tragedy this misfortune would
have been a punishment; here it is an opportunity for Ahab to choose good
or evil: temptation to the Christian hero is an opportunity for grace. It is
in making the wrong choice initially and persisting in wrong choices that
Ahab refuses grace and brings punishment on himself. Therefore Auden can
say about the Christian hero that suffering leads to self-blindness, defiance,
and hatred; of Shakespeare's tragedies he asserts that they might be termed
"variations on the same tragic myth, the only one which Christianity possesses, the story of the unrepentent thief."[39]

A very carefully constructed theory of Christian tragedy is that of
Preston T. Roberts, Jr., who is oriented towards the Neo-Aristotelian
"Chicago" school of criticism. But since the *Poetics* came out of the context of Greek theology there are in it, says Roberts, theological elements to
which the Christian must of necessity object, particularly "the notion of
God as an ideal rather than as an actual entity, the divine spectator alone
with himself thinking about thought, viewing the course of events without
passion from above and beyond and apart; the notion of man as a primarily
intellectual and sensitive as opposed to a passionate and wilful being, a being
whose inherent nobility is imprisoned within a bodily and emotional frame;
and an emphasis upon the aesthetic and intellectual as opposed to the moral,

the political, and the religious virtues."[40] The Christian view also is to be differentiated from the modern skepticism which denies God and human responsibility; plays displaying this mentality comprise, along with the Greek and Christian, a third type of drama, Roberts maintains.

Out of the Greek milieu grew Aristotle's concept of the tragic hero, which is too aristocratic for the Christian, and the interpretation of hamartia as an intellectual mistake rather than a moral sin, which is peculiarly Greek. Then Roberts moves to answer the familiar objections that Christianity lifts man beyond tragedy, and that therefore other forms of drama (e.g., the epic and the comic) more fully deal with the Christian story.

The first objection arises, Roberts maintains, from a theological misconception which fails to take into account the fact that there is always a hiatus between the theological possibility and the human actuality, which is that no one rises too high to fall, or falls too low for redemption. Roberts's own theological immanentism would also clash with such a transcendental approach. He believes that "the Christian story as a whole and in all its parts is wholly concerned with something within this given and actual world and does not involve any essential reference beyond life and history to another possible or impossible one." On the other hand, the Christian play, as he sees it, is not purely a realistic event but a symbolic joining of "what is actual in this life with what is possible for it and what is possible for this life with what is actual in it."

The second objection to Christian tragedy arises from too narrow a notion of what tragedy is, Roberts asserts. Tragedy is not purely tragic, not merely despair and doom; some tragedies "turn upon the theme of man's idolatry and pretension rather than upon the theme of man's suffering nobility or piteous abnormality. They move from fate to freedom, from defeat to victory, from doom to grace, and from tragedy to peace."[41]

As for the Christian tragic hero, he is modeled on Christ and is related both to the world and to other people in a way in which the towering and solitary Greek tragic hero, modeled on the removed and transcendent Greek deity, is not. But there are also moments when the Christian tragic hero is free to consider or ignore himself, others, the world, or God. By dint of this freedom he is susceptible to moral guilt and religious sin. The misuse of freedom constitutes his hamartia or flaw, whereas the Greek tragic hero is ignorant or finite, and the modern skeptical play would have its protagonist perverted, inert, or weak. Also, because of the intellectual nature of Greek hamartia, the discovery scene of Greek tragedy will probably come after the tragic deed, not before it. In the Christian play the flaw is a matter of guilt and sin, not ignorance; therefore the recognition scene precedes the tragic deed. In the course of the play, the Christian tragic hero moves in the recognition scene "from knowledge, through temptation, to sin" and in the reversal "from judgment to forgiveness." This is a movement beyond tragedy only in the sense that he experiences joy even in the midst of agony and pain. To the Greek, however, there is no salvation within history, no good news—he dies like Oedipus, "unreconciled to the real God or life and history." Similarly, the modern skeptical hero dies "defiant, weary, and melancholy, cursing the day wherein he was born."[42]

The plot of the Christian play is, in contrast to the fatal and determined Greek play, "open" at the beginning, middle, and end. It has a real beginning, with "relevant possibilities and real alternatives in the initial situation." There is a real middle: "the individualities involved in a Christian plot begin as effects facing the past and end as causes facing the future." And there is a real end: "There is an appropriation of the dead by the living. What is divested of living immediacy becomes immortal by presenting itself to what follows as a final or persuasive cause and by determining what is to follow as an efficient or coercive cause. In this sense every beginning is an end, and every end is a beginning. . . . The end is therefore more than a denouement or something after which there is nothing. In losing his life, the tragic hero finds it." The effect of the Christian play is neither the pity and terror of the Greek nor the poignance and despair of the skeptical play but "a sense of judgment and forgiveness": judgment, for "the tragic deed has involved moral guilt and religious sin and because the consequences of the tragic deed are often less than this specifiable guilt and sin"; forgiveness, for "a conjunction between God's grace and man's repentance and faith in part redeem that which has been betrayed and forsaken."[43]

Theology also influences the function of foils and the chorus. In the Greek play only the tragic hero, solitary and transcendent, one against the many, is likely to be round; the minor characters are flat. But to Christianity all men are children of God; therefore all the characters, common and uncommon—even the porter in *Macbeth,* the fool in Lear, the soldiers in *Henry V,* are alive, are "terribly real and moving at some point and moment, undergoing their own tragedy and finding their own peace."[44]

Whereas Preston Roberts patterns his discussion of tragedy on the *Poetics,* Roger L. Cox looks also to tragic writers from the Christian era to ascertain how Christianity has altered the "complexion of tragedy." Nevertheless, early in the book he offers a tentative definition of tragedy as

a literary work, predominantly somber in tone, in which the main character encounters some significant misfortune for which he himself is partly, though not wholly, responsible. . . . That is to say, tragedy deals basically with the timeless problem of necessary injustice; and since it involves the *mis*fortune of a person who is at least partly good, rather than with anyone's *unmerited good* fortune, it deals with necessary suffering. The human condition is such that when human suffering is seen in a literary work to be the product of absolute necessity, it affords some insight, some liberation—if not to the hero, at least to the audience.

Most theoreticians of tragedy have gone wrong, Cox continues, in their understanding of the term *responsible,* for they have viewed the action of the protagonist as a sufficient cause of the misfortune, and therefore see him as blameworthy. Cox, on the other hand, views the action of the protagonist as merely a necessary cause, and therefore does not place the blame on him for his suffering. The second problematical term is *necessary.* Cox denies that there is "no way out" for the protagonist; he could choose a way out of his dilemma, but to do so would be to deny his own essential nature. Oedipus, for instance, must seek for the knowledge that will ruin him, "since the knowledge that he feels compelled to pursue *is* the knowledge of his own identity."[45] If this is true, there is no point in looking for some "flaw," as Aristotle did, simplistically assuming that the good act well and are happy, and that suffering proves that one is guilty in some way. The character and crucifixion of Christ fit Cox's definition perfectly, and the Gospel paradigm makes the tragic view acceptable to Christianity. Christ acted freely so as to fulfill his prophesied role as victim; to do otherwise would have been impossible for him. Yet his actions were part of a larger cosmic scheme. His voluntary and reluctant taking of suffering on himself constitutes a liberating transcendence of suffering.

Within the Christian tradition Cox discerns two strains of thought, the Pauline and the Johannine, corresponding to Western and Eastern Christendom respectively. The two differ in respect to their interpretation of sin, law, judgment (or justification), and the concept of time. The Pauline writings treat sin as the deadly force that controls the unregenerate individual, from which he cannot extricate himself but must be delivered by a new birth. The Johannine writings see sin as "an offence against the light" of Christ, i.e., the delusion of self-sufficiency, which blinds the unbeliever and leaves him in spiritual darkness; evil is the "by-product" of unbelief.

For Paul the law is the Mosaic Law, which is important for the Christian only because he is unable to obey it and is condemned by it; only the grace of God can deliver him. John, on the other hand, sees the Law not as something superseded by grace but as prefiguring Christ and being fulfilled by him. For Paul justification is recreation of the individual in Christ. For John judgment is cast in cosmic-apocalyptic images; Christ the light-bringer will defeat the Prince of darkness, and those who believe in him will participate in his victory. Finally, Paul sees salvation taking place in time; he traces the rejection of the truth by the Jews and its subsequent revelation to the Gentiles. For John salvation is not a matter of past and future history but takes place now, in a "continuous present."[46]

Cox discusses selected plays of Shakespeare and the major novels of Dostoyevsky as illustrative of these two perspectives. Shakespeare, as a Westerner, displays Pauline themes in his tragedies. The problem of Hamlet's flaw, his inability to obey his father's ghost, parallels Paul's description in Romans 7 of man's inability to obey the Law of God, and the play is full of military images that play on the etymology of *hamartia* as "missing the mark," failing to hit what one sets as his target. *Lear* is analyzed by reference to Paul's concept of self-love, especially in I Corinthians. Lear is deceived by flattery; Goneril and Regan are motivated by lust; only Edgar and Cordelia show charity. Cox's discussion of *Macbeth* begins with the citation of the drunken porter's speech, in which there are several references to Satan. Cox, alluding to the Gospel of Luke, views Macbeth as "divided against himself" so that his kingdom cannot stand.

Dostoyevsky is, according to Cox, the great successor to Shakespeare as a writer of Christian tragedy, but his works reflect the Johannine emphasis of Russian Orthodoxy. The story of the raising of Lazarus from John 11, which Sonya reads to Raskolnikov in the middle of *Crime and Punishment*, explains the ending of the novel. As Martha, Lazarus' sister, had to believe before her brother was revived, so Sonya's belief makes possible Raskolnikov's rebirth; as in the Gospel, the new life is not described for us. The "apocalyptic vision" of Prince Myshkin in *The Idiot* is analyzed in terms of three allusions in the novel; the condemned man about to be executed perceiving an "eternity of life"; the epileptic's feeling of joy and harmony just before his seizure; and participation in the redemptive suffering of Christ. All three of these experiences are timelessly present in the Johannine sense. *The Idiot* also contains major images from Revelation which reenforce the presentation of the Prince's vision as a spiritual new creation. Likewise the language and imagery of the "Grand Inquisitor" chapter of *The Brothers Karamazov* recall the description of the "false prophet" in Revelation, and his charges against Christianity are effectively answered in the character of Father Zossima.

To conclude, Cox advances several assertions about the nature of Christian tragedy, among them the following:

1. The "law of retaliation" is replaced by the "law of love," which precludes returning evil for evil. Characters are called upon to recognize that if people were treated as they deserve, everyone would deserve ill treatment, as Hamlet tells Polonius in Act II.

2. The family is redefined. No longer are blood relationships paramount, as in Greek tragedy; instead, one's responsibility is to all men, even one's enemies. Lear recognizes this, and so does Alyosha in *The Brothers Karamazov.*

3. There is stress on the "reciprocal concepts of love" rather than the static categories of moralism. Heaven and hell are not "places" for the "good" and "bad" people; the spiritual condition of love or hatred is what is important in the characters, as Sonya illustrates.

As a kind of postscript, we should consider the very scholarly and systematic approach to tragedy taken by T.R. Henn, particularly his discussion of hubris, tragic death and rebirth, and the tragic effect, as he relates them to Christianity. Henn denies the distinction sometimes made between Greek metaphysical hubris and Christian moral hubris. Drawing on the theology of Reinhold Niebuhr, Henn claims that for Christianity as well as tragedy, hubris is not ethical but metaphysical, inherent in man's finitude: "man as spirit transcends the natural and temporal process in which he is involved and also transcends himself. Thus his freedom is the basis for his creativity but it is also his temptation." When man attempts to deny his finitude, he blinds and deceives himself, and conflict arises which produces suffering.[47] This can be seen in such differing tragic protagonists as Antigone, Faustus and Faust, Macbeth, and Peer Gynt, each illustrating Niebuhr's observation in his own way.

But this one similarity does not imply that tragedy can be regarded as a substitute for religion, for religion posits, as Karl Jaspers recognizes, "worlds beyond tragedy." A better way to regard the relationship between tragedy and Christianity, Henn feels, is to look at tragedy as a lesser analogy to Christianity in terms of their patterns of death and rebirth, and their effect on the spectator. The ending of tragedy shows a resolution of tragic conflict between the creature and his creaturehood: see, for example, Lear's "Prithee, undo this button," Creon's call to a cabinet meeting at the end of Anouilh's *Antigone,* the Chorus's last lines in the *Hippolytus* and *Samson Agonistes,* or Charmian's last lines at the end of *Antony and Cleopatra.* Yet the resolution is not final but projects, "out of the unification which it suggests, the sense of continuity and re-birth." This is of a lesser order, but in some sense it is complementary to the Christian belief in immortality. Finally, the tragic stimulus to pity and fear is parallel to religious experience. "The awakening of pity seems the first step ... to a sense of Christian charity: that of fear, a necessary state of mind to our readiness to consider the idea of the numinous; both together forcing us to confront a series of ethical problems which have their solution only in faith." Pity and fear also turn us outward from our egocentricity and involve us in compassion and co-suffering. Compassion, or co-suffering, is a response which is central to Christianity, because the redemption of mankind was motivated by Christ's love, "itself the last perfection of compasssion."[48]

The Comic

There is less theological speculation about comedy than about tragedy, but, as with tragedy, many critics express the idea that the Christian religion and comedy are incompatible. Reinhold Niebuhr, who objected to the idea of Christian tragedy, makes a similar case against Christian comedy. Humor is a response to the immediate incongruities of life, he observes; we judge, but we exercise mercy and merely laugh at the fool playing the part of a king or at the indignity of a proud man. We are able to do so because we can stand, psychologically, at a distance from the situation and perceive congruity at a higher level: it is poetically just that the fool be king, and that a proud man lose his dignity. The distance that allows laughter at others is also possible when we judge ourselves but refuse to take ourselves too seriously; a sense of humor is a sign of self-transcendence and freedom in the human spirit. But we can not laugh at the ultimate incongruities of life or at our own evil, from which laughter is impotent to free us. In such serious matters laughter can only lead to bitterness. What is efficacious is not the tentative resolution of mercy and justice in humor, but the final judgment of God on our sins, and the ultimate mercy of God in spite of our sins: the resolution of these is only at the Cross. Laughter at best, then, is a preparation for prayer, and humor a preliminary to faith.[49]

Similarly Kenneth Hamilton, who follows Northrup Frye in associating comedy with summertime growth and with the defeat of what is conceived to be only ugly, not deadly, reasons that comedy "is not ultimately serious, as tragedy is; and this is because it does not face—and cannot face from its intrinsic limits—the ultimate of death. Therefore, while it has much to say (fairly seriously) on the moral and social level, it has nothing whatsoever to say on the religious level." Christianity has to do with deadly evil, and victory is won at the cost of the Crucifixion.[50]

Another critic who opposes the notion of Christian tragedy, E.I. Watkin, sees Christianity as utterly serious, not comic. Commenting on T.S. Eliot's *The Cocktail Party,* he writes: "If comedy is seen in the light of religious truth, the spectacle of man's immortal spirit in its relation to the eternal God, only the superficial comedy of circumstance or manners remains to amuse us. The deeper comedy of characters, of perversity, inconsistency and folly, ceases to be comic." On the surface Eliot's play is a drawing-room comedy, but the central moral choice, that of Celia, leads to a martyr's death, and is comic only in a Dantean sense.[51]

Among those theorists who do hold that Christianity and comedy are compatible there seem to be two lines of thinking. P.T. Forsyth sees the comic as an exaltation of man's mind or spirit over his body, his worldliness. As noted in chapter four, Forsyth relies on the aesthetic of Hegel, from whom he has learned that Christian art produced two new features: (1) the tendency to the fantastic, the exuberant, and the childish (like the spouts of cathedrals), which passes into (2) the grotesque or the humorous. In ancient comedy, which tended toward satire, there was little humor. The tone was intellectual and dry rather than sympathetic or extravagant. The humor of Christian drama, in contrast, is "of a loving, sympathetic, and pitiful sort; the wit does twinkle, it does not merely flash; and the laugh lies much nearer to the spring of tears than anything antiquity can show. The hard gaiety of the old world is replaced by kindly humour in the new."[52]

This alteration in humor, as Forsyth sees it, can be traced to three sources: (1) a new power and freedom infused by Christianity into the human spirit, bringing with it a new disposition to revel, free from the restraints of taste and law, for the sake of mere fun; (2) a new sense of sympathy and kindness that men experienced in feeling they were redeemed, no longer dogged by mysterious Fate or avenging Furies; and (3) a new sense of the greatness of God, of life, of the soul: "The world's pettiness at one moment irritates us, and at another, measured against the world's vast and blessed issues, it moves us to a smile, now tender only, now tender and grim (as in Carlyle). United in spirit ourselves with the Infinite and Eternal, we see the trivialities of life as Gulliver watched the Lilliputians climbing over his boots."[53]

Unlike Forsyth, who stresses the comic as a transcendence of the human condition, the other Christian commentators on comedy stress, in various ways, the involvement of the comic in the human, the physical, and the earthly.

W.H. Auden, who differentiates, as we have seen, between Greek and Christian tragedy, makes a similar distinction between classical and Christian comedy which recalls Forsyth in some respects. Classical comedy, observes Auden, was relatively narrow in scope, being based on the sociological division of man into "those who have *arete* and those who do not." Only the latter, "fools, shameless rascals, slaves," are proper for comedy. A Christian society is a much more amenable environment for comedy, allowing it more breadth and depth. It allows for more breadth because Christianity believes that all men are sinful: "no one, therefore, whatever his rank or talents, can claim immunity from the comic exposure and, indeed, the more virtuous, in the Greek sense, a man is, the more he realizes that he deserves to be ex-posed." It allows for more depth because Christianity forbids looking down on others and judging them; it enjoins forgiveness and does not support the classic practice of exposing the comic rascals. Therefore, Auden notes, when the classical comedy ends the audience feels superior to the characters and laughts *at* them, while with Christian comedy the members of the audience, realizing that they too are sinners, are sympathetic and laugh *with* them.[54]

The approach to comedy of William Lynch, like that of Auden, eschews the class division of ancient comedy and with it the "division of styles," by which, according to Erich Auerbach, the common, the ordinary, the "realistic" were reserved for the comic low style, which was not felt to have serious depth.[55] Lynch's view is precisely the opposite: for him comedy deals with the common, the ordinary, the finite more concretely and more densely than does any other art—even more than tragedy, which can dissolve into nihilism or heroism as an escape from finitude. The perspective of comedy is to diminish; it makes what it focuses on "a disconcertingly small puddle" but closely scrutinizes "the actual contours, the interstices, the

smells, of the beastly man." For instance, there is the inescapable realism
of Prince Hal when in *1 Henry IV* he speaks of Falstaff as "that trunk of
humours, that bolting hutch of beastliness, that swoll'n parcel of dropsies,
that huge bombard of sack, that stuff'd cloakbag of guts, that roasted
Manningtree ox with the pudding in his belly, that reverend vice, that grey
iniquity, that father ruffian, that vanity in years."[56]

Comedy thus destroys man's "angelic" pretensions, his sophistications,
his claims to pure intelligence. It also ridicules his "pseudocomic" roles.
There is the Chaplinesque self-pitying clown, who cannot survive the victory
of man implied by the resurrection. There is the meticulous and fastidious
man, as George Bernard Shaw reveals himself to be when he ridicules
churches in Italy, and specifically "the average Italian priest, personally un-
cleanly, and with chronic catarrh of the nose and throat, produced and
maintained by sleeping in frowsy, ill-ventilated rooms, punctuating his
gabbled Latin only by expectorative hawking, and making the decent guest
sicken and shiver every time the horrible splash of spitten mucus echoes
along the vaulting from the marble steps of the altar: this unseemly wretch
should be seized and put out, bell, book, candle, and all, until he learns to
behave himself."[57] There is the Sartrean man who belches with disgust at
the world; such is Puck in *A Midsummer Night's Dream,* who is interested
in transforming the human into something else—usually worse. Finally,
there is the diabolical *poseur* who hates the human and laughs at what is
ultimately serious; such a one is Thomas Mann's Adrian Leverkuhn, who
lives only on the intellectual level and makes fun of everything.

In short, comedy is a kind of *amnesis,* a remembrance of our contin-
gency, our fallenness and createdness before God.[58] It works this remembrance by disrupting our so-called rational notions of pattern and logic.
Whereas the tragic is ruthlessly logical (the tragic hero moves to full awareness in a tight step-by-step process), comedy recalls the relation of man to
God without such logic—and is therefore funny. There are two ways, says
Lynch, that comedy takes to accomplish this. The first way is to fore-
shorten the process by omitting intervening steps and fostering surprises;
so that he observes: "Let us not talk of incongruity as the secret clue to
comedy, but of congruity, of the tie between the earth and Christ, with all
the logic omitted. Why should we laugh or magnify the Lord? Because this
is the way things are." Or it multiplies the steps between the beginning and
the end; thus "the bewildering vitality of the finite, within the analogical
form, goes beyond the logic of tragedy and everything is seen as lively and

extraordinarily bouncing."[59]   This is the Rube Goldberg technique.

In "The Bias of Comedy and the Narrow Escape into Faith," Nathan A. Scott, Jr., expatiates on Lynch's theory. He disagrees with Lynch, in passing, about the comic nature of the clown; of Charlie Chaplin's *The Tramp,* for example, he claims that "we feel that here is the real human thing itself—clothed not in the unearthly magnificence of tragic heroism but in the awkward innocence of essential humanity." But the definition of the comic which Scott proposes is clearly indebted to Lynch:

The comic is a contradiction in the relation of the human individual to the created order of existence; this contradiction arises out of an over-specialization of some instinct or faculty of the self, or out of an inordinate inclination of the self in some special direction, to the neglect of the other avenues through which it ought also to gain expression. . . . However, in the comic action, this contradiction in the individual's relation to the created orders of life does not involve the spectator in suffering or pity, for he is not led to identify with the protagonist who, indeed, in the course of the action becomes the butt of his laughter.

To the type of comic hero who is unsympathetic, like Volpone or Tartuffe or Dostoyevsky's "underground" man, Scott would add a second type. Don Quixote and Joyce Cary's Gulley Jimson (from *The Horse's Mouth*) suggest a type of comic protagonist who is heroic and admirable. The nature of the comic catharsis, which involves "such a restoration of our confidence in the realm of finitude as enables us to see the daily occasions of our earth-bound career as being not irrelevant inconveniences but as possible roads into what is ultimately significant in life," is determined by the type of comic protagonist. If he is unsympathetic, "our awareness of the validity of the human norm from which he has deviated will be renewed and deepened as we see him rendered incompetent by this eccentricity." If he is sympathetic, "the experience of katharsis grows out of the joy we take in the discovery of how stout and gamy the human creature really is."[60]

Scott also explicitly connects this idea of comedy to the doctrines of Creation and Incarnation. The comic confidence in the finite grows, for the Christian, out of his belief that the world was made by God and is therefore, despite man's sinfulness, essentially good. It is also separate from God, a created thing and therefore not "defective" in that it is finite. Into this created world God himself entered, submitting himself to it and thus affirming the value of its materiality and particularity, and also affirming the image of his creature, man, to whose image comedy also, in its way, attests.

Both kinds of comic theory discussed above—the adjectives "transcendental" and "immanent" might be used to differentiate between them—have been called into question by contemporary drama that does not appear to be amenable to Christian theorizing. Some modern comedy approaches, even closer than tragedy, the brink of nihilistic despair, and can be used to make this nihilism endurable; this may be why, E.J. Tinsley speculates, many today prefer this kind of farcical comedy. He cites Friedrich Dürrenmatt, who considers comedy the only sort of drama suited to a disbelieving age; it is "a means of learning to face life without any standpoint. Man is no longer seen to have tragic possibilities—that would imply some transcendental reference—and is a pathetic being whose state can best be presented through a new use of the comic routine."[61]

The traditional comedy, which makes one more deeply aware of "the natural norms of human life," is contrasted by Nathan A. Scott, Jr., to contemporary "absurdist" comedy, which comes out of a world where all norms are questionable. This strange new comedy reaches toward the fearsome universe of tragedy and the unbalanced universe of farce; "the dance of comedy becomes, in other words, a *danse macabre*, and the critics who persist in trying neatly to distinguish between the tragic and the comic modes of art end by simply going mad."[62]

We would have been left with the critical antinomy between transcendence and immanence, as well as the inability to deal with "absurd" and "black" comedy, were it not for the work of Nelvin Vos, which fits these issues into a larger theological framework. Vos argues that the task of the Christian theorist of comedy is to examine the relationship between the Christian story, which is essentially the action of the Christ, and the action typical to comedy. First, he notes that there are three traditional foci on the action of Christ: (1) the focus on Christ the Victor, the kingly Messiah, the miracle worker, the raiser of the dead, the one who rose from the dead and ascended into heaven and who will come again in glory and judgment; (2) the focus on Christ the Victim, the Suffering Servant, the lowly and unrecognized, the betrayed and rejected, the Sacrificial Lamb slain for the sins of the world; and (3) the image of Christ which presents both Victim and Victor together, the New Testament stress on the kenotic Christ's self-emptying and resultant exaltation.[63]

In these three images of Christ's action we have clues to the patterns of comedy sufficient to explain the contradiction between theories of comedy emphasizing transcendence and those emphasizing immanence, and to provide insight into modern nihilistic comedy as well. Vos does not attempt to generalize about all comedy at once, as other critics have done; instead, he delineates three patterns of comic action corresponding to the three images of Christ's action. Each type of comedy assumes a different world-view as well as a pattern of purpose, passion, and perception on the part of the comic protagonist.[64]

The pattern of comic action which Vos identifies as "The Structure of the Comic Victor" involves an optimistic attitude towards man's place in the world, and stresses his rationality and triumph over difficulties. The movement of the comic victor is as follows: "Because, in the first part, the protagonist experiences little or no suffering or passion, in the second part there is nothing to hinder his gaining a perception of an all-encompassing purpose at work in his universe. In the third part, the protagonist triumphs and is victorious over the world's obstacles, not because he has actually chosen or accomplished a significant action, but in spite of his foolishness. Therefore, the fortunate and sociable world of the comic victor is an optimistic world."[65]

Vos identifies the comic victor with the traditional "wit." The wit is able to see, from a position of superiority, what is ludicrous and absurd; he is the one who is amused when he sees another person slip on the banana peel or make a fool of himself; indeed, he can be a practical joker and arrange for the other's fall, or he can merely engage in verbal wisecracks. From a position of strength and pride he detachedly observes the follies of his fellows.[66]

This pattern, which seems to resemble what P.T. Forsyth had in mind in his "transcendental" theory of comedy, is exemplified in the Greek and Roman comedies, in Shakespeare's early work such as *A Comedy of Errors* and *A Midsummer Night's Dream,* in eighteenth-century sentimental comedy, and in the work of George Bernard Shaw, William Saroyan, and Thornton Wilder, whose writing Vos submits to detailed analysis. In Wilder we see a tone of festivity and good fortune; difficulties and pain are not dominant, and there is no basic incongruity between man and his universe.

A second pattern of comic action is "The Structure of the Comic Victim." The comic victim is identified with the age-old "butt," who *receives* the ludicrous and the absurd; he is the one who falls on the banana peel, who is passive, who feels infirm, weak, and trapped.[67] The comic victim, too, is involved in a tripartite movement: "Because in the first part no purpose appears to be at work in the protagonist's world, in the second part he arrives at the perception of an all-embracing suffering or passion as the dominant and pervasive quality of life. In the third part, the protagonist is defeated and victimized, because his actions are insignificant and meaningless. Therefore the empty and isolated world of the comic victim is an absurd world."[68] Thus Vos is able to make critical sense of a kind of comedy which puzzled Tinsley and Scott. Cited as examples of this drama is the "dark comedy" of Molière, Ben Jonson, and Chekhov, as well as of the dramatists of the "absurd" such as Samuel Beckett, Pirandello, Genet, Adamov, Dürrenmatt, and Ionesco, whose plays are discussed at length. In contrast to Wilder, Ionesco portrays a world in which the dominant mood is hellish: pain, suffering, and death are dominant, and there is a basic incongruity within man and between man and man, as well as between man and the universe.

Such an incongruity is also evident in "black humor," which reveals man threatened by being reduced to an object, a machine. This is the case, for instance, with Mr. Zero in Elmer Rice's *Adding Machine*, with Willy Loman in Arthur Miller's *Death of a Salesman;* it appears in the more recent work of Thomas Pynchon, J.P. Donleavy, Vladimir Nabokov, John Barth, Terry Southern, James Purdy, Bruce Jay Friedman, and Joseph Heller. In Heller's *Catch-22*, Major Major and the other characters are all attempting to resist being made into things, into military numbers.[69]

But neither the comic victor nor the comic victim does justice to the full Christian story. The comedy of the victor resembles Dante's version of Paradise, characterized by knowledge, agape love, and joy; the comedy of the victim resembles the Inferno, where there is only self-love, isolation, and the absence of the infinite. The full Christian story is constituted by the complete journey of Dante, whose spiritual center is not the perfection of pure infinity or the horror of pure finitude but their meeting point in the Purgatorio, where there is purgation through grace leading to reconciliation. The comic action which is analogous to the complete pilgrimage of the Divine Comedy, and to the entire story of Christ as well, involves the passage from victim to victor. The movement of the comic victim-victor is also in three parts: "Because, in the first part, the protagonist is convinced that purpose is at work in his world, in the second part, when he experiences suffering or passion, he is put to the test for his conviction. In the third part, he arrives at a new perception of both defeat and triumph, not in spite of his imperfection, but because he has mortified himself and has consented to acknowledge that he is a victim of sin and guilt. Therefore, the sin-ridden and gracious world of the comic victim-victor is the world of faith."[70] This "Structure of the Comic Victim-Victor" is evident in such plays as Shakespeare's *Measure for Measure* and the modern comedies of T.S. Eliot and Christopher Fry.

For Fry festivity and sacrifice, despair and hope are interrelated. Furthermore, the relationship between the infinite and the finite is a complex one. The infinite becomes involved with the finite, grace comes to meet man in his predicament and deliver him from it. It is in this kind of comedy, I think, that the observations of Lynch and Scott are borne out: the finite is fully affirmed as the place where the infinite is experienced. Thus both the immanent and the transcendent are joined in one comic form.

The protagonist of the drama of the comic victim-victor is related by Vos to the traditional figure of the clown, who, unlike the wit, is able to accept the absurd and the ludicrous, and can laugh at himself when he slips on the banana peel. He humbly accepts his finitude and his kinship to other people; thus is introduced the possibility of love. At the same time, unlike the butt there is in the clown a strong drive for survival and self-preservation; he displays the "amazing versatility of bouncing upright again." But the clown is also the sufferer, on whom the spectators place their own short-comings, and he is a liberator, for he "magically frees us from the bondage of both gravity and finitude, of taking our own abilities too seriously and our frail condition too lightly." He is, in Saint Paul's words, a fool for Christ's sake; to take the comparison further, he "is" Christ, who is also the scapegoat and the liberator.[71]

Harvey Cox, in an essay on "Christ the Harlequin," follows Vos by pointing out that one of the earliest pictures of Christ shows a crucified man with the head of an ass, and that the biblical Christ is also suggestive of the clown: "Like the jester, Christ defies custom and scorns crowned heads. Like a wandering troubadour he has no place to lay his head. Like the clown in the circus parade, he satirizes existing authority by riding into town replete with regal pageantry when he has no earthly power. Like a minstrel he frequents dinners and parties. At the end he is costumed by his enemies in a mocking caricature of royal paraphernalia. He is crucified amidst sniggers and taunts with a sign over his head that lampoons his laughable claim."[72] It is true, Cox continues, that not all periods of Christian history have looked on Christ in this way. Why, then, does this perspective find favor in an age of genocide and the threat of global annihilation? Because the clown transcends the bounds of normal human propriety and possibility, and thus offers a model for hope.

CHAPTER SIX

THEOLOGIES OF PLAY AND CHRISTIAN CRITICISM

In an essay which surveys literary and theological criticism, Giles Gunn lists three ways in which literature can be regarded as religious. First, we are unable as readers to give full assent to the hypothetical situations literature presents to us unless they are commensurate with our "deepest sense of ourselves." Our sensibilities, however, are also extended by imaginative literature. Second, the experience of a work of literature is analogous to the religious experience of reality as ultimate, for we perceive in the work of literary art some ultimate orientation, some intuition about what constitutes the ground of experience. Thirdly, literary works are hypothetical creations, and they assume on our part acceptance of "vital possibilities," the element of "More" beyond the limits of immediate perception.[1]

We can see these three emphases throughout theological literary criticism, but I would suggest that what Gunn labels the "More," the sense of "vital possibilities" beyond the realm of the empirical, is of special interest at the moment. Two sorts of considerations influence the directions of theological criticism. First, there is the nature of literature itself; for example, the presence of symbols and the differentiation of genres lead Christian Critics to discuss symbolism and the relation of the Christian story to tragedy and comedy. Second, the characteristics of theology must be noted. Christian Critics reflect the emphases of particular confessional traditions, so that a Roman Catholic or Anglican, for instance, is likely to stress the Incarnation or the sacramental implications of poetry. No doubt confessional traditions will continue to shape criticism of literature, but there seem also to be dominant trends in theology at certain times; witness the popularity of theologies of culture and the more recent "secular" theology. Presently in theological circles there seems to be a reaction across confessional lines against secularism and immanence, and a new affirmation of the long-discredited transcendent. In the larger world to which theologians respond, this reaction is most markedly evident in the "counter culture," which is attuned to the emotional and sensual rather than the rational, the mystical rather than the manipulatible, the aesthetic and religious rather than the economic and political, the celebrative rather than the serious.

But despite the pronouncements of a "new consciousness" by such men as Theodore Roszak, Norman O. Brown and Charles Reich, the only example of such an approach among literary critics I have noticed is a call by Leslie Fiedler for a "new new criticism" to replace the analytical, rational, antiromantic New Criticism which was aimed at the age of T.S. Eliot, Proust, Joyce, and Thomas Mann. We are now, however, in a postmodernist age which is Dionysian and romantic, and the new new criticism, according to Fiedler, should deal not with the analysis of words on a page but "words in the head, at the private juncture of a thousand contexts—social, psychological, historical, biographical, geographical—in the consciousness of the reader (delivered for an instant, but an instant only, from all those contexts by the *ekstasis* of reading)." In this postmodernist age there are new sorts of literature to be criticized, too. Fiedler designates three types: the Western (but this time the "red man" beats the white man, in such works as John Barth's *The Sot Weed Factor,* Ken Kesey's *One Flew Over the Cuckoo's Nest,* and Leonard Cohen's *Beautiful Losers*); Science Fiction (Burroughs's *Nova Express,* Golding's *Lord of the Flies,* Burgess's *Clockwork Orange,* Barth's *Giles Goat-Boy*); and Pornography (Hubert Selby's *Last Exit to Brooklyn,* Terry Southern's *Candy,* Philip Roth's *Portnoy's Complaint,* John Updike's *Couples*). This recent literature crosses the border between the "cultured" and the "uncultured," as well as closing the generation gap; it also goes beyond the "real" to the mystical, the marvelous, the fantastic, the transcendent. Once more literature evokes the dream, the ecstatic vision; it is once again "prophetic and universal—a continuing revelation appropriate to a permanent religious revolution, whose function is precisely to transform the secular crowd into a sacred community, one with each other and equally at home in the world of technology and the realm of wonder." Matthew Arnold was correct, therefore, in seeing poetry as the basis for religion in the future, but he could never have imagined what either the new poetry or the new religion would be like.[2]

Coinciding, however, with the reaction against scientific rationalism and the emphasis on the sensuous and mystical is a widespread emphasis on transcendence and play which seems promising for the Christian Critic. Transcendence is a difficult concept to define; among contemporary theologians the preoccupation does not seem to be with a transcendent deity (as, say, was characteristic of the early Karl Barth) but with man's experiences of the transcendent, of that which is above and beyond the ordinary, the mundane, the natural. In Peter Berger's *A Rumor of Angels,* the publication of which has been viewed as the event which locates the new theology,[3] the author sets out various human gestures which he sees as "signals of transcendence." Two of these signals have been attested to by much literary criticism, Christian and otherwise, in the past half century. The tendency to order, to endow human existence with structure and meaning, has often been seen by critics as central to man the maker of verbal constructs or mythopoeic patterns. The signal of damnation, the outrage at offences which not only cut the offender off from the normal human community but seem to require a supernatural curse, is witnessed to by much existential literature. The other signals have only during the past few years been the subjects for critical concern. The tendency to hope has been central for contemporary eschatological theology, and the signal of humor is the theme for the new interest in comedy and celebration. The one other signal of transcendence, the urge to play, is the focus of attention in the new theology of play.[4]

The first theologian to make a careful study of play was the German Jesuit Hugo Rahner, who traced the concept from Plato to Aquinas to establish its importance in Western Christian thought. God is seen as the supreme Player, and the universe His plaything, created not out of necessity but out of divine freedom and delight. With this in mind the ancients, and the Christian mystics as well, sometimes pictured the creator as a child playing with the world. Man, the "toy" of God, is to imitate the joy and beauteous lightness of the creator, not in a spirit of frivolity but as the "grave-merry" man who is possessed of the virtue of *eutrapelia* advocated by Aristotle in the *Nicomachean Ethics* and reasserted, despite the puritanical sternness of many of the Church Fathers, by Aquinas. *Eutrapelia* is the Latin *humanitas;* it is "a kind of mobility of the soul, by which a truly cultured person 'turns' to lovely, bright, and relaxing things, without losing himself in them: it is, so to speak, a spiritual elegance of movement in which his seriousness and his moral character can be perceived." The Christian can achieve such a balance between seriousness and distance from the world because he both loves the world into which Christ was incarnated, and looks beyond it, in the spirit of childlike trust, to the eternal delight of Paradise, the "divine children's game" and "dance of the spirit."[5]

Rahner has some interesting things to say about how art fits into the cosmic-human rhythm of play. For one thing, play *is* art, imitation of reality; yet we can only learn through imitation what reality is. The fact that games are important in life should not then be unexpected. Furthermore, art (in the narrow sense of painting, poetry, etc.) longs for the divine; all artists are "possessed by the spirit, who in sound, in colour or by gesture, venture the attempt of uttering the unutterable, and who, in that rare moment, seem suddenly, though but for an instant, to have attained their desire, feel playing around them the smile of divinity, the smile that is a reflection of the Divine Wisdom playing upon the earth."[6] Indeed, artistic harmony and pattern participate in the larger cosmic dance which the ancients recognized in the movement of the stars, the pattern which was symbolized in the solemn movements of the liturgy and in the subliturgical dances which the authorities were never able to remove from the Christian church.

Harvey Cox[7] traces the loss of festivity and fantasy as represented in the medieval holiday of misrule. Festivity is the excessive revelry which oversteps the bounds of the ordinary and historic; fantasy is the ability to envision extraordinary possibilities, breaking the rules and structures of everyday reality. Festivity and fantasy are valuable because they free man from the practical and allow him to see "broader and more subtle dimensions" of life. In the light of festivity and fantasy, traditional Christian theology is too oriented to the past, modern "secular" theology is too limited to the present, and the theology of hope (eschatological theology) is too exclusively directed to the future. Cox advocates a theology of juxtaposition which will recognize but transcend these limitations, and make possible a more imaginative theology. The image of "Christ the Harlequin" is helpful here, for it juxtaposes fatalism and optimism, disillusionment and hope.

Unlike Rahner, David L. Miller[8] takes Plato and Aristotle to task for subordinating play to the serious and initiating the disastrous division between the two which has plagued Western thought. But beginning with nineteenth-century Romanticism, feeling and play were once again recognized, and in twentieth-century literature and criticism, "play" and "games" are important. We may indeed live in a time when play is our mythos, our basic metaphor. In an essay entitled "Play Is Religion" Miller sketches out four dimensions of a mythology of play: (1) *aesthesis,* spiritual or imaginative knowing which opens up the senses to wonder; (2) *poiesis,* the creation of fictions and the recognition that the cosmos must be understood in terms of the imagination; (3) *metamorphosis,* or change: the player sees that stability is found only in change; and (4) *therapeia,* the working together of the other functions towards an attitude of "unserious" openness to wonder and mystery. Miller concludes by advocating play as the root metaphor for the religion of the future: faith will be the "poesy of make-believe."

Sam Keen, in *Apology for Wonder,* sees that man has lost his sense of the celebrative. Traditional man, *homo admirans,* accepted the cosmos as a meaningful gift to which he should respond with contemplation and joy. Modern man is labeled *homo faber,* for he no longer discerns unity and meaning in the cosmos but feels he must fabricate his own universe by manipulating his environment. Both these mentalities in the extreme are pathological. Traditional man ran the risk of disregarding necessity and limit; modern man's rationality destroys freedom and celebrates only itself. Keen argues that man needs both wonder and rationality; he should be *homo tempestivus,* timely man, who must both trust the world and be willing to act in it. For the religious person wonder is based on belief in a ground of being and a confidence to act appropriately in the world. Keen's second book, *To a Dancing God,* is less positive about the traditional religious posture, which he sees as possibly unavailable for modern man. This is especially the case with Christianity, with its insistence on authoritative revelation in the past and its emphasis on passive hearing of the "Word." This is all too abstract and intellectual, for man's perceptions of the world are basically physical, and any relationship with the ultimate or the sacred must be the result of bodily experience, symbolized for Keen in the dance.

Robert Neale treats the subject from a psychological point of view. From Schiller, Neale takes the idea that man's psyche is dualistic, needing both to discharge energy and design experience. If the first predominates, man turns towards the concrete and immediate and spontaneous; if the second predominates, the general and the abstract are stressed. When these tendencies clash we have "work" to resolve the conflict; when they harmonize we have "play." Psychic conflict and work are identified as "profane," whereas psychic harmony, which gives the individual the creative advantages of both power and form, Neale labels "sacred." Religion, then, is defined as the "full play" response to the harmonious experience of the sacred.[9]

All of these writers, William Dean generalizes in a recent study, assert the pre-eminence of play, but their metaphysics are sketchy, and they do not spell out the theological implications of what they are doing. Dean's purpose is to offer a full systematic apologetic for the celebrative experience, which he describes in aesthetic terms as "beauty." He argues that those experiences which have traditionally been held to be of prime importance are, in fact, means to something else. Only the experience of beauty is in itself satisfying; it is not directed to mere truthful reiteration of reality, or to the future results of ethical behavior, or to the remoteness of the holy, but provides novelty and significance in the present.

To provide a philosophical rationale for beauty, Dean draws on Whitehead's theory of reality as process. In this view what is actual is not the past, which cannot be captured, or the future, which has not yet arrived, but only the immediacy of the present. Only experience as it is felt in the present, then, can be seen as valuable. Dean then goes on to describe three stages in the experience of reality: there is initially the sensation of physical data, then the initial interpretation of the data, then a final decision about how to deal with the interpretation. The initial reception of sense data is called "reality," and the mental interpretation is called "appearance," for which the individual uses either natural symbols of sense perception or conventional symbols such as language or music. He can construct from reality theories or propositions, or he can mentally feel propositions by "propositional feelings." Dean makes these distinctions in preparation for his Whiteheadian definition of the aesthetic experience, or beauty, as occurring "whenever there is a contrast between reality, or how the individual receives his past, and appearance, or how an individual mentally construes his past."[10] This experience is intrinsically valuable because it is immediately satisfying—it provides "zest" and adventure—and it further demands that one either accept or reject the new interpretation of reality. This definition has several implications: beauty is not restricted to "artistic" objects such as paintings or poems; and what contrasts with accepted reality at one point in time may subsequently fail to do so.

Dean then relates beauty to goodness, truth, and the holy. Beauty is related to ethics in the sense that the ethical aim is to provide a beautiful object for the future. Beauty is related to truth both positively and negatively: truth can keep beauty "honest" to the way things are, but excessive concern with truth can prevent the emergence of the new. Beauty is related to the experience of the holy if God is defined as the source of the novelty necessary for the aesthetic experience. The experience of newness, in other words, is the experience of the "superjective" nature of God as he presents "potentialities" to man which were not previously actualized. God therefore is known in all experiences of beauty, not just in some special revelation; also, the experience of the holy is relative to the individual subject and to his cultural context. Finally, while truth may call to mind past experience of God, and morality may be directed to future experience, the experience of present aesthetic contrast between appearance and reality "provides the situation for the actual experience of God."[11]

If the religious experience is basically aesthetic, it follows that the theologian should be interested in the "commotion" found in the contrast between reality (the traditional) and newness. The religious experience, in fact, is defined as the contrast between the sacred "appearance" (a new personal vision of experience) and the profane "reality" (the accepted version of how things are); the sacred in itself is esoteric and incomprehensible, while the profane by itself is repetitive and dead—only in the interplay between them is life enlivened and revolutionized.

Clearly Dean has gone further than the other theologians of play in giving a rationale for "beauty"; his definition of beauty, though, is so broad as to encompass all that is usually implied by the words creative, innovative, imaginative, etc.—anything which is not traditional. Impatient with churchy Christianity, Dean looks to the artistic and political arenas for the aesthetic excitement he seeks. Yet the terms "God" and "grace" and "salvation" still come to his mind in connection with the beauty which is ultimately satisfying; he has sacralized the traditionally profane, and judged the traditionally religious to be profane.

The theologians of play often end their books with projections and hints that they think are deserving of detailed development in the future. I would like to be very tentative, too, at this point, and merely outline what I sense to be the advantages for Christian Critics in this new theology.

1. A close relationship between the poetic imagination and the religious imagination is assumed. There is no desire any longer to rationalize or demythologize the faith, but there is the aim to treat positively the areas of myth, fable, drama, and metaphor. On the other hand, there is no hint that the new theologians want to place religion in some sacrosanct realm apart from the world. Even the "correlation" by the theologians of culture of two separate realms of truth, the religious and the cultural, seems to be for-

gotten. As the incarnationists and sacramentalists showed that the concrete is the means of grace, as Tillich demonstrated that the so-called secular has the dimension of depth, so the new theologians perceive that what at first appears to be serious is ultimately playful.

2. The new theology and the complementary literary criticism, of which Fiedler's essay is perhaps a foretaste, would be more inclusive than criticism has sometimes been in the twentieth century, especially in America, although Fiedler's claim that criticism should not be directed to "words on the page" introduces an unfortunate limitation into his program. The super-analytical experience, the "words in the head" in the "thousand contexts" Fiedler has in mind, should supplement, not replace, the close reading the New Critics have taught us: the "new new" criticism should be as catholic as possible.

3. Criticism making use of the insights of the new theology may be better able to come to grips with the contemporary literature that Fiedler mentions. Until now theological critics have usually been uncomfortable with the new forms, or they have ignored them as beneath their dignity to recognize. Such an attitude would be impossible for a critic "turned on" by the new theology! Such hitherto neglected aspects as fantasy, magic, the occult, as well as pornography, might be opened up.

The possibilities are as endless as movements in the great cosmic dance so often alluded to, if theological critics will dare to become players in an exciting game whose rules have yet even to be dreamed up.

NOTES

Chapter One

1. Tillich, *Systematic Theology*, I:27.
2. *Complete Works of Percy Bysshe Shelley*, ed. Roger Ingpen and Walter E. Peck, VII:112.
3. Arnold, *Literature and Dogma*, pp. 13, 11, 46, 70; and *Essays in Criticism, Second Series*, ed. S.R. Littlewood, p. 1.
4. See Irving Babbitt's "Humanism: An Essay at Definition," *Humanism and America*, ed. Norman Foerster.
5. Eliot, *Selected Essays*, 3rd ed.
6. Eliot, "Second Thoughts about Humanism," *Selected Essays*, pp. 486-487.
7. Eliot, *Selected Essays*, pp. 17, 21-22, 31, 24.
8. Eliot, *Selected Essays*, pp. 17-19, 137.
9. Eliot, *On Poetry and Poets*, p. 221.
10. Eliot, *After Strange Gods*, pp. 11-12, 63; *Selected Essays*, p. 388.
11. Eliot, *The Use of Poetry and the Use of Criticism*, pp. 95-96.
12. Eliot, *On Poetry and Poets*, pp. 250, 264.
13. Eliot, "Rudyard Kipling," *On Poetry and Poets*, p. 292; "Baudelaire," *Selected Essays*, pp. 421, 427, 430.
14. Bentley, *The Importance of Scrutiny*, p. xxii; Leavis, *The Common Pursuit*, pp. 212-213.
15. Bentley, pp. 286, 278.
16. Since Every was, according to Amos N. Wilder (*Theology and Modern Literature*, p. 85) poetry editor for Eliot's journal *The Criterion*, it is safe to assume, I think, that Eliot's later criticism influenced the development of Every's own critical theories.
17. Leavis, p. 254.
18. Bentley, p. 397; Buckley, *Poetry and Morality*, p. 233.
19. Bentley, p. 91.
20. Every, "The Necessity of Scrutiny," *Theology* 38 (March 1939): 177, 183-184.

21. Every, *Christian Discrimination,* pp. 11, viii.
22. Lewis, "Christianity and Culture," *Theology* 40 (March 1940): 169-170; Every, "In Defence of Criticism," *Theology* 41 (September 1940): 162-163. This argument anticipates the defense of literature on the basis of natural theology, which will be discussed in detail in chapter two.
23. Every, *Christian Discrimination,* pp. 65, 47, 10-11.
24. Every, *Poetry and Personal Responsibility,* pp. 74-84.
25. She writes in a review entitled "Charlotte Yonge and 'Christian Discrimination'" that "the tendency of orthodoxy is to repress these perceptions ['the finest and keenest perceptions of an age' expressed in literature—which may not be orthodox] for its own convenience and cause a moral cramp in the developing consciousness" (*Scrutiny* 12 [1943]: 159).
26. Every, *Poetry and Personal Responsibility,* p. 73.
27. Bethell, "Christianity and Culture: Replies to Mr. Lewis," *Theology* 40 (May 1940): 357; and *The Literary Outlook,* p. 6.
28. Bethell, *Essays on Literary Criticism,* pp. 24-25.
29. Bethell, *The Literary Outlook,* pp. 83-87.
30. Bethell, *The Literary Outlook,* p. 101.
31. Bethell, *Essays on Literary Criticism,* pp. 21-22.
32. Stallman, "The New Critics," *Critiques and Essays in Criticism: 1920-1948,* ed. R. W. Stallman, p. 496; Tate, *Essays of Four Decades,* pp. 619, 206.
33. Nathan A. Scott, Jr., *Modern Literature and the Religious Frontier,* p. ix; Tate, pp. 554, 172, 44.
34. Tate, pp. 8, 11.
35. Tate, pp. 13, 9, 16.
36. Brooks, "Criticism, History, and Critical Relativism," *The Well-Wrought Urn,* pp. 215-219.
37. Brooks, "Metaphor and the Function of Criticism," *Spiritual Problems in Contemporary Literature,* ed. Stanley R. Hopper, pp. 134-135. I might add that the mythic nature of religion and poetry is thematic in the work of John Crowe Ransom as early as *God Without Thunder.* But I am not aware that he indulges in explicitly theological criticism in the manner practiced by Tate and Brooks.
38. Brooks, "Christianity, Myth, and the Symbolism of Poetry," *Christian Faith and the Contemporary Arts,* ed. Finley Eversole, p. 105.
39. Brooks, *The Hidden God,* p. 5.
40. Brooks, *The Hidden God,* p. 97.
41. From Tillich's *Theology of Culture,* quoted on p. 7 of *The Hidden God.*
42. Brooks, *The Hidden God,* pp. 15, 99, 132.
43. John Macquarrie, *Twentieth-Century Religious Thought,* pp. 171-172; Hulme, *Speculations,* ed. Herbert Read, 2nd ed., pp. 8, 71. Hulme attaches several sets of labels to this pair of opposing attitudes. He terms the view of which he disapproves "romanticism" or "humanism," and his own view he calls "classical" or, as the passages cited demonstrate, "religious." He associates such names as Pelagius and Rousseau with the former, and such names as Saint Augustine, Aquinas, and Pascal with the latter.

Hulme's adherence to the "religious" or "classical" position resulted in definite aesthetic pronouncements; he predicted a decline in artistic concern with human feeling and form, and a new interest in abstract, geometric, even mechanical forms which would subordinate the organic and vital. That this position leads him to conclusions about aesthetics is perhaps the exception rather than the rule in the tradition to which Hulme allies himself. Saint Augustine, for example, and Pascal, as well as their modern disciples whom we shall encounter in this discussion—such figures as the theologian Karl Barth and the critic W.H. Auden—tend to have a negative opinion of man's culture in general and of his art in particular as inventions of a depraved creature and therefore possessing minimal religious value.

44. Hugh Ross Mackintosh, *Types of Modern Theology*, pp. 150-151, 191.
45. Barth, *Der Römerbrief.* The sixth edition was published as *The Epistle to the Romans.* These references are to pp. 56, 167-168 of the English translation.
46. Barth's later work, especially *The Humanity of God,* is less scathing. But this does not diminish the influence that Barthian theology of the post-World War I period had against the earlier theology, an influence in Protestant thought which parallels the influence of Hulme in literary criticism.
47. Hulme, pp. 51-52; Niebuhr, *The Nature and Destiny of Man,* I: 93, and *An Interpretation of Christian Ethics,* pp. 14-15; Scott, *Modern Literature and the Religious Frontier,* p. v.
48. Auden, *The Dyer's Hand,* pp. 456-457.
49. David E. Roberts, *Existentialism and Religious Belief,* pp. 67, 69-71.
50. Tillich, *Systematic Theology,* I: 62-63, and *Theology of Culture,* p. 42.
51. Macquarrie, p. 279; Maritain, *The Degrees of Knowledge.*
52. *Theology* 41 (July 1940): 29-30.
53. Ramsey, *An Era in Anglican Theology,* pp. 16, 2-3; Temple, *Nature, Man and God,* pp. 306, 493.

Chapter Two

1. Quoted in David Cairns, "Natural Theology," *A Handbook of Christian Theology,* ed. Marvin Halverson and Arthur A. Cohen, p. 251.
2. Maritain, *Creative Intuition in Art and Poetry,* pp. 48-49.
3. Maritain, *Creative Intuition,* pp. 3, 115, 97.
4. Maritain, *Art and Scholasticism and The Frontiers of Poetry,* pp. 66, 132.
5. Maritain, *Art and Scholasticism,* p. 139. The clear separation of art and poetry from grace leads Amos N. Wilder to place Maritain with W.H. Auden (*Modern Poetry and the Christian Tradition,* pp. 11-12). But nowhere does Maritain share Auden's attitude that poetry is for the Christian "small beer." Indeed, as Nathan Scott points out, Maritain's attitude is very similar to that of the New Critics ("Maritain in His Role as Aesthetician," *The Review of Metaphysics* 8 [March 1955]: 480-492).
6. Cf. Maritain's remark that the aesthetic virtues (of humility and integrity) imitate the virtues of man as man and are analogous to the Gospel virtues (*The Responsibility of the Artist,* pp. 99-100).
7. Gardiner, *Norms for the Novel,* pp. 99, 104-106, 109-110, 138-139.
8. See Gardiner, *Fifty Years of the American Novel,* and *In All Conscience.*
9. Turnell, *Poetry and Crisis,* pp. 6-7, 141-142.
10. Turnell, *Poetry and Crisis,* pp. 76, 57, 77.
11. Machen, *Hieroglyphics,* pp. 160, 162-163.
12. Root, "Beginning All Over Again," *Soundings,* ed. A.R. Vidler, pp. 3, 5, 19. This is a volume meant to continue the tradition of collections of essays which have provided the direction for Anglican divinity for over a century. Vidler, in his introduction, lists these collections: *Essays and Reviews,* 1860; *Lux Mundi,* 1889; *Foundations,* 1912; *Essays Catholic and Critical,* 1926 (p. x).
13. Root, p. 18; Michael Roberts, "The Moral Influence of Poetry,"

Theology 39 (January 1939): 25.
14. Strong, *The Great Poets and Their Theology*, p. vii.
15. Wilder, *Modern Poetry and the Christian Tradition*, pp. 18, 20.
16. Pottle, *Christian Teaching of Literature*, p. 6.
17. Scott, "Faith and Art in a World Awry," *The Climate of Faith in Modern Literature*, ed. Nathan A. Scott, Jr., p. 6; Walker, *A History of The Christian Church*, p. 17.
18. Harned, *Theology and the Arts*, pp. 149, 153, 167.
19. Tillich, *The Religious Situation*, pp. 53-54, 70, xi-xii (Niebuhr's preface as translator).
20. Luccock, *Contemporary American Literature and Religion*, pp. 166,176.
21. Wilder, *The Spiritual Aspects of the New Poetry*, p. 3.
22. Wilder, *Modern Poetry and the Christian Tradition*, and *Theology and Modern Literature*, p. 85.
23. Tillich, *Systematic Theology*, I: 218, 12.
24. Tillich, *The Interpretation of History*, p. 50, and *Systematic Theology*, I, 13.
25. Tillich, *Systematic Theology*, I: 63.
26. Tillich, *The Protestant Era*, p. 67, and *Theology of Culture*, pp. 74, 70. Tillich's analysis of "depth" has not gone unquestioned. Roger Hazelton is severely critical of him at this point: "Any work of art is both expressive and impressive and so must be reckoned with on both counts. This, I believe, is where Paul Tillich's view of the relation between religion and art sadly fails us. He does not provide us with anything like a perspective for Christian discrimination because he thinks of the art work as wholly expressive and judges it accordingly. His conception of a 'religious style' comes remarkably close to that of German expressionism. . . . The work of art is for Tillich an ontological tool or token; it is not, however, a seal or pledge of reality in the Christian sacramental sense" (*New Accents in Contemporary Theology*, p. 22).
27. Tillich, *Theology of Culture*, p. 68.
28. Hazelton, *New Accents in Contemporary Theology*, p. 15.
29. Scott, *Modern Literature and the Religious Frontier*, pp. 28, 30-31, 33, 38-39.
30. Scott, *Modern Literature and the Religious Frontier*, pp. 47-48. Scott has reference to Buber's famous book *I and Thou*. Scott has updated his thesis that "the world of literary experience is a personalist universe, a world of dialogue" in "Criticism and the Religious Frontier," *Humanities, Religion, and The Arts Tomorrow*, ed. Howard Hunter, pp. 47-52.
31. The principle here, as Scott points out, is the Incarnation, seeing the Divine Ground through conditioned realities. I shall discuss this principle further in chapter three, below.
32. Scott, "The Relation of Theology to Literary Criticism," *Journal of Religion* 33 (October 1953): 271-272.
33. Luccock, pp. 130, 9, 10.
34. Wilder, *Spiritual Aspects of the New Poetry*, p. 196, and *Modern Poetry and the Christian Tradition*, p. 259.
35. Holthusen, "What is Christian in a Christian Literature?" *Christian Faith and the Contemporary Arts*, p. 99.
36. Vahanian, *Wait Without Idols*, p. 246. See also his *The Death of God*, pp. 134-155.
37. Altizer and Hamilton, *Radical Theology and The Death of God*, pp. 11, 139-155, 171-191.
38. Hamilton, *The New Essence of Christianity*, and *Radical Theology*, p. 92.

39. Scott, "The Crisis of Faith in the New Theology and the Promise of Grace in Poetic Art," _The Broken Center,_ pp. 145-186.
40. See Scott, "Theology and the Literary Imagination," _Adversity and Grace,_ where he traces the secularity of modern biblical scholarship and theology, noting that though the death-of-God thinkers want a "Gospel without God," what the most incisive minds are communicating is that God is to be found in the _midst_ of historical experience.
41. Scott, _Negative Capability,_ pp. 6-11.
42. Scott, _Negative Capability,_ pp. 36, 43.
43. Scott, _Negative Capability,_ p. 47. He adds Kurt Vonnegut, Jr., William Burroughs, Donald Barthelme, and Norman Mailer (_An American Dream_) when he launches an attack, along similar lines, on the new "apocalyptic" counter-culture sensibility which abandons the world and escapes to a mad interiority. (" 'New Heav'ns, New Earth'—the Landscape of Contemporary Apocalypse," _Journal of Religion_ 53 [1973]: 1-35.)
44. Cf. the much less hopeful essay regarding the "new" literature, "Beckett's Journey into the Zone of Zero," in Scott's _Craters of the Spirit._
45. Scott, _Negative Capability,_ pp. 66, 81, 83, 85. From a strictly theological perspective, John S. Reist, Jr., also advises waiting. Citing Barth's concept of divine "patience," God's allowing independent existence and development of creatures as He waits in judgment or mercy, Reist counsels the theological critic to "admit that Paradise has been lost, but that the temporal-spacial aspect of reality might itself be testimony to the willingness of God to wait for his creature as he wanders through the modern corridors of time from empty cistern to empty cistern." As he waits, however, the critic should not be over-anxious to "baptize" non-Christian literature ("Treading Water in the Acheron: A Study in the Nature and Function of Theological Literary Criticism," _Christian Scholar's Review_ 2 [1972]: 216-217.)

Chapter Three

1. Gerald F. Else, _Aristotle's Poetics: The Argument,_ pp. 1-2.
2. John H. Randall, Jr., _Aristotle,_ pp. 274-275. The "quotation" from Aristotle is Randall's conjecture. It is perhaps relevant to note here that the ancient Greek version of the Old Testament, the Septuagint, uses forms of _poieō_ in its rendering of the Genesis account of Creation, as does the New Testament when it refers to God as Creator (see, e.g., the Greek of Acts 4:24 or Romans 1:20).
3. Spingarn, _A History of Literary Criticism in the Renaissance,_ 2nd ed., pp. 157-158; Anthony [Ashley Cooper, Third] Earl of Shaftesbury, _Characteristicks of Men, Manners, Opinions, Times,_ 5th ed., I: 207; Coleridge, _Biographia Literaria,_ ed. John Shawcross, I: 202.
4. William K. Wimsatt, Jr., and Cleanth Brooks, in their _Literary Criticism: A Short History,_ trace this passage back through Herder to Shaftesbury's _Moralists_ (p. 374, n. 8). Wellek cites Schelling as the source of much of Chapters XII and XIII of the _Biographia;_ see _A History of Modern Criticism,_ II: 152. D.G. James claims that Coleridge, following Kant, held that "the imagination is creative in ordinary perception; for it is primarily due to its activity that what is given as sensation is synthesized together into wholes, so that we become aware of objects interacting and thereby themselves unified into larger." The secondary imagination, which Coleridge describes as an "echo" of the primary imagination, then breaks down the percep-

tions synthesized from the ordinary world to build up an artistic world (*Scepticism and Poetry,* p. 24).

5. Van der Leeuw, *Sacred and Profane Beauty,* pp. 286-7, 280-81, 285.

6. Cf. T.S. Eliot's theory of creative "depersonalization" discussed in chapter one. Cf. also Berdyaev's assertion that "creative genius is not concerned with salvation or perdition. In his creative work the artist forgets about himself, about his own personality, and renounces himself. Creative work is intensely personal and at the same time it means forgetfulness of self. Creative activity always involves sacrifice" (*The Destiny of Man,* 2nd ed., p. 130). But creativeness is not directly moral, Berdyaev warns: the creator does not, as creator, feel humility or a sense of sin; in short, the self-sacrifice of creative genius is not directed towards moral improvement or salvation, though it is necessary for God's work in the world. See below for a fuller exposition of the idea of creativeness.

7. Berdyaev, *Dream and Reality,* p. 209.

8. Berdyaev, *The Meaning of the Creative Act,* p. 129. Roger Hazelton, in *A Theological Approach to Art,* more modestly sees the analogy between God's Creation and artistic creation as a vital process: "When we read the Genesis accounts, especially that given in the second chapter, we must agree with Gerhard von Rad that the narrative 'moves not so much between poles of nothingness and creation as between the poles of chaos and cosmos' [*Genesis: A Commentary,* p. 80]. This is because in Genesis the accent falls so heavily upon God's action in creation rather than upon his absoluteness or self-containment of being. Creation does not happen all at once, nor is it entirely one complete and single act; God calls, forms, distinguishes and names the multifariousness of the world" (p. 53).

9. Berdyaev, *Creative Act,* pp. 225, 142, 246, and *The Destiny of Man,* pp. 126, 128. According to Harned, Berdyaev sees the realm of primeval freedom, the *Gottheit* or *Ungrund* (terms borrowed from the medieval mystics Meister Eckhart and Jacob Boehme), to be outside God and the Source of man's freedom. Thus "man's freedom cannot be called the gift of the Creator. Like divine freedom, it evolves from the Ungrund; its powers for creation and destruction are neither controlled nor wholly known by God. He calls man to engage in the transfiguration of the tragic potentialities of this primordial freedom and in the creation of the greatest possible meaning and value. But he cannot coerce. Man is his partner, not his pawn" (*Theology and the Arts,* p. 83).

10. Van der Leeuw, p. 290. Roy W. Battenhouse makes nearly the same point when he writes that "good" poetry necessitates an accurate vision by which the poet perceives the complexity of his experience and integrates it into "a larger body of myth." In biblical terms, the poet "should be able, like Adam in the Garden, to name every creature correctly. Apprehending the form of each thing that is brought before him, he should be able to assign it its proper place." But Battenhouse goes on to say that this accuracy is rare among poets because they, like other men, have lost the original Adamic innocence and need the restorative power of the Christian myth to afford them the proper perspective ("The Relation of Theology to Literary Criticism," *Journal of Bible and Religion* 13 [February 1945]: 20).

11. The famous philosopher of culture Ernst Cassirer advances a similar theory, stating that "humanity really attains its insight into objective reality only through the medium of its own activity and the progressive differentiation of that activity; before man thinks in terms of logical concepts, he holds his experiences by means of clear, separate, mythical images." Language performs a comparable pre-logical function, for "the limits of things

must first be posited, the outlines drawn, by the agency of language; and this is accomplished as man's activity becomes internally organized, and his conception of Being acquires a correspondingly clear and definite pattern" (*Language and Myth*, p. 37).

12. Schwartz, "The Vocation of the Poet in the Modern World," *Spiritual Problems in Contemporary Literature*, p. 61.

13. Jacques Maritain, "The Experience of the Poet," *The Situation of Poetry*, Jacques and Raissa Maritain, pp. 77-79.

14. Tinsley, "The Incarnation and Art," *The Church and the Arts*, ed. Frank J. Glendenning.

15. These are not new ideas. Spingarn, in his *Literary Criticism of the Renaissance*, states that both Petrarch and Boccaccio argue that "theology itself is a form of poetry—the poetry of God. Both of them insist that the Bible is essentially poetical, and that Christ himself spoke largely in poetical images." Spingarn continues by emphasizing that this last point is much stressed by Renaissance critics (pp. 8-9).

16. W.H. Auden uses this "hiddenness" of Christ to argue that no Christian can feel comfortable as an artist. The artistic impulse is expressive, and tends towards manifestation; but the coming of Christ, paradoxically, is hidden except to faith, which is not generated by imagination but by grace. Auden writes that "the Incarnation, the coming of Christ in the form of a servant who cannot be recognized by the eye of flesh and blood, but only by the eye of faith, puts an end to all claims of the imagination to be the faculty which decides what is truly sacred and what is profane. A pagan god can appear on earth in disguise but, so long as he wears his disguise, no man is expected to recognize nor can. But Christ appears looking just like any other man, yet claims that He is the Way, the Truth, and the Life, and that no man can come to God the Father except through Him. The contradiction between the profane appearance and the sacred assertion is impassible to the imagination" (*The Dyer's Hand*, p. 457). This is essentially a Kierkegaardian-Barthian argument.

17. Knight, *The Christian Renaissance*, 2nd ed., pp. 49, 53, 52.

18. Bradner, *Incarnation in Religion and Literature*, pp. 7-8; TeSelle, *Literature and the Christian Life*, pp. 158-159. Bradner also analyzes the literary structure of Saint Luke's Gospel briefly, but a much more detailed approach to the Gospels has come to be associated with the British theologian Austin Farrer, whose studies of imagery resemble the American New Criticism. See below, chapter four.

19. Van der Leeuw, pp. 324-325, 327, 339-340.

20. Scott, *Modern Literature and Religious Frontier*, pp. 51, 55. He also mentions Tate's "The Angelic Imagination: Poe as God" and Maritain's *The Dream of Descartes*.

21. Scott, *Modern Literature and Religious Frontier*, pp. 61-62.

22. Lynch, *Christ and Apollo*, pp. 8-12, 113, 158.

23. Lynch, pp. 116-117, 187. See the essay on the "Concrete Universal" by W.K. Wimsatt, Jr., in *The Verbal Icon*.

24. Scott, *Modern Literature and Religious Frontier*, p. 63. Elman's title is "Twice-Blessed Enamel Flowers" (an allusion to J.D. Salinger's short story "De Daumier-Smith's Blue Period," in which the protagonist, after living in a fanciful romantic dream world, comes to a grateful appreciation of the natural world). The essay is in *The Climate of Faith in Modern Literature*. Auerbach's subtitle is *The Representation of Reality in Western Literature*. One of his main theses is that for the ancient Greeks and Romans serious literature eschewed the commonplaces and specifics of life, which were

relegated to comedy and farce. But it was the Hebrew-Christian tradition (the Prophets and the Christ were common men, but the ordinariness and concreteness of their lives were ultimately significant), which came to the fore in the Middle Ages, that lay behind modern realistic literature and allowed seriousness, tragedy, and spiritual depth to the everyday and the common. Amos Wilder expands on Auerbach's thesis, stressing the historical-narrative forms of the Old Testament, and setting up several characteristics of the Hebrew epos which he regards as part of the religious context in which the theological critic may judge literature: (1) the making of order out of the chaos of life; (2) realism, the "rich dense portrayal of human experience"; (3) the stylistic emphasis on verb and action, response and confrontation that involves the issues of freedom, responsibility, loneliness, and shame—in contrast to a stylistic emphasis on the descriptive adjective, and psychological subjectivism. Most modern literature, he goes on to say, is fragmented and partial in light of these criteria (*The New Voice*, pp. 41-77).

25. TeSelle, pp. 114-115.
26. Berdyaev, *Creative Act*, p. 138.
27. Berdyaev, *Creative Act*, pp. 110, 99, 323, and *Dream and Reality*, p. 295.
28. Sayers, *The Mind of the Maker*.
29. A.C. Bridge, in *Images of God*, comes to a similarly trinitarian model from the opposite direction. He speaks of the work of art as *symbolic*, i.e., as the focal point of the "coming together" of the transcendent reality and material thing (p. 24). A third aspect of the "symbolic process" is the observer, who is challenged to respond (the power of challenge has been called the Holy Spirit [see pp. 139-145]). Sayers moves from theology to an understanding of the artistic process; Bridge moves from a schematization of the artistic process to an understanding of the Trinity.
30. Sayers, pp. 37-38.
31. Sayers, pp. 39-40.
32. Sayers, pp. 40-41.
33. Sayers, p. 151. Direct imposition of Idea closely resembles the "angelism" of the New Critics and Lynch's "univocal" imagination. The "Son-ridden" poet possesses what resembles the "equivocal" imagination described by Lynch, but Sayers's explanation seems the more satisfactory of the two. Lynch follows the New Critics in their desire for rich poetic texture; there is some question, however, whether poetry that could be adjudged weak in texture (e.g., much eighteenth-century verse) is therefore bad. Perhaps Lynch's criteria work best for metaphysical or modern poetry but not so well with other styles.
34. Almost a decade later a much more renowned writer, Denis de Rougement, suggested a very similar trinitarian theory of "the human mysteries of the act of art." What he merely outlined, though, had already been treated in detail by Sayers. De Rougement's proposal appears in his essay "Religion and the Mission of the Artist," *Spiritual Problems in Contemporary Literature*, pp. 183-185.

Chapter Four

1. Ross, *Poetry and Dogma,* pp. 10-11, 27. In much less sophisticated terms, Hugh McCarron, S.J., in *Realization* advances a similar theory of the relationship between poetry and sacrament: "a poem dimly resembles the sacraments in this, that it is also an attempt to portray things, active things in a real way. Moreover, the sacraments are signs. Our words too are signs to symbolize, finally, not a general statement of truth, but rather things in act, in which truth ultimately resides. Thirdly, poetry unites the lower creation, soil, air, rain, plant, animal with truth in man, in God. Christ the Word of God, the Son of Man, does this. His sacraments do it. Poetry, in a way far less important than the supernatural sacraments, does it" (p. 84).

2. Ross, p. 53.

3. Ross, pp. 228, 18, 246.

4. Wilder, "Christianity and the Arts: The Historic Divorce and the Contemporary Situation," *Christian Scholar* 40 (December 1957): 265-266.

5. Jones, "Art and Sacrament, " *The New Orpheus,* pp. 29, 34. Here Jones's theory closely resembles that of Susanne Langer in *Philosophy in a New Key,* which designates such characteristic activity as "symbolic."

6. In the sense of natural theology.

7. Jones, pp. 46-47, 40, 45.

8. Jarrett-Kerr, "Dostoyevsky and the Agony of Belief," *Studies in Literature and Belief;* Scott, *Rehearsals of Discomposure,* p. 98; Elman, p. 100.

9. Scott, *The Wild Prayer of Longing,* p. 28.

10. Scott, *Wild Prayer,* p. 71.

11. Forsyth, *Christ on Parnassus,* p. 84.

12. Forsyth, pp. 257-258.

13. Krumm, "Theology and Literature: The Terms of the Dialogue on the Modern Scene," *The Climate of Faith in Modern Literature,* p. 24. For a discussion which stresses religious and literary theories of symbolism see Donald Scott Heines, "Problems of Literary Criticism and Theological Perspectives" (unpublished dissertation, Columbia University, 1964). Heines deals with figures who appear in this study, but he also treats several whom I do not discuss in detail: Martin Buber, Philip Wheelwright, Erich Auerbach, and W.K. Wimsatt, Jr. However, he makes little attempt to "place" theological criticism in a context of literary criticism and theology, and focuses on less than a dozen "major" critics.

14. Battenhouse, "The Relation of Theology to Literary Criticism," p. 20.

15. Scott, "Religious Symbolism in Contemporary Literature," *Religious Symbolism,* ed. F. Ernest Johnson, pp. 159-184. Since Scott introduces the theology of Tillich into a discussion of symbol and myth in literature, it is perhaps appropriate at this point to mention Tillich's views on these subjects. One of the characteristics of symbol to Tillich is its "power of opening up dimensions of reality." The difference between artistic symbols and religious symbols is that the former "open up the human spirit for the dimension of its intrinsic meaning," whereas the latter "mediate ultimate reality through things, persons, events which because of their mediating functions receive the quality of 'holy' " ("The Meaning and Justification of Religious Symbols," *Religious Experience and Truth,* ed. Sidney Hook, pp. 4-5). Elsewhere Tillich writes that the work of art as a figurative thing "does not point beyond itself to a reality of a different order." It rather "expresses wholly intrinsically the reality it aims to express." Thus art is to be distinguished from myth, which is "an objectification of the transcendent through the medium of intuitions and conceptions of reality." When art

tries to express transcendent reality (as, for instance, in symbolic art) it sacrifices its purely artistic character and takes on symbolic and mythic character ("The Religious Symbol," Hook, pp. 312-313). Here Tillich would seem to be with the New Critics, who insist that a work of art not be dissolved into something else but must be looked at as a self-contained whole. However, we have seen Tillich introduce the religious dimension of "depth" in his theology of culture and in his discussion of artistic styles (see above, chapters one and two).

16. H.D. Lewis, *Morals and Revelation,* pp. 208-209, 212.

17. H.D. Lewis, pp. 215-216.

18. H.D. Lewis, p. 255.

19. Brett, "The Function of Literary Imagery," *Christian Scholar* 36 (June 1953): 96. The modern New Testament criticism to which Brett evidently refers has come to be known as "the theology of images," and is a movement, primarily among British Anglo-Catholic scholars, to apply what appears to be the techniques of the New Criticism to the Bible, and to undergird the practical criticism with theoretical statements about the significance of image and symbol for the Christian revelation. See Austin Farrer, *A Glass of Vision,* and *A Rebirth of Images,* as well as Eric Mascall's *Words and Images* and *Theology and Images.*

20. See, for instance, Martin Jarrett-Kerr's questioning of the Jungian approach of Maud Bodkin. He sees two problems with it: (1) the racial unconscious is highly indiscriminate; (2) it is doubtful whether universal archetypes can reestablish the possibility of affirmation of images, for among the experiences basic to man is "the pull and interplay between fact and fiction, which evaporates if it is itself treated as fiction" (*Studies in Literature and Belief,* p. 176).

21. Hepburn, "Poetry and Religious Belief," *Metaphysical Beliefs,* ed. Alasdair MacIntyre, p. 98.

22. Bultmann, "New Testament and Mythology," *Kerygma and Myth,* ed. Hans Werner Barsch, pp. 17-44.

23. Frye, *Perspective on Man,* pp. 33-41; Wilder, "Scholars, Theologians, and Ancient Rhetoric," *Journal of Biblical Literature* 75 (1956): 10-11, and "Poetry and Religion," *Christian Faith and the Contemporary Arts,* p. 114.

24. Van Buren, *The Secular Meaning of the Gospel.*

25. Berdyaev, *Freedom and the Spirit,* pp. 54, 61.

26. Berdyaev, *The Meaning of the Creative Act,* pp. 226, 228, 240, 247-248. In his distinction between classic and Christian art Berdyaev is possibly influenced by German romantic criticism: Wellek quotes August Wilhelm Schlegel as making a very similar distinction between Greek and "Romantic" poetry (*A History of Modern Criticism,* II: 59).

Chapter Five

1. This is the thesis of Gerardus van der Leeuw in *Sacred and Profane Beauty.*

2. In the twentieth century, however, there has been an effort to reverse the trend and once again write religious drama. I am thinking especially of the British playwrights stimulated by the annual Canterbury Festivals beginning in 1929. William V. Spanos, in his book *The Christian Tradition in Modern British Verse Drama: The Poetics of Sacramental Time,* sees these playwrights (e.g., Charles Williams, T.S. Eliot, John Masefield, and Christo-

pher Fry) attempting to portray the insights of Anglican incarnational-sacramental theology by writing plays which display the unity of past, present, and future, and the unity of flesh and spirit.

3. Watkin, *Poets and Mystics,* p. 41.
4. Richards, *Principles of Literary Criticism,* p. 246.
5. Jaspers, *Tragedy Is Not Enough,* p. 35.
6. Jaspers, pp. 38-39.
7. Sewell, *The Vision of Tragedy,* pp. 51-55.
8. Niebuhr, *Beyond Tragedy,* p. 163.
9. Niebuhr, *Beyond Tragedy,* pp. 155-156. Henrietta Ten Harmsel similarly believes that tragedy only approximates Christianity, though she credits the writers with a true, if partial, vision of the human condition. She reviews Aristotle's criteria: the completeness and magnitude of the tragic action; the characteristics of the hero (nobility, descent from fortune, flaw—regarded either as taking on of guilt or the fatal attempt to introduce perfection into an imperfect world); the arousing of pity and fear in the observer, and subsequent purgation. The Christian story is complete and possesses magnitude; Christ more than fulfills the classical role of the hero; and the believer is spiritually purged. Furthermore, the Crucifixion, even more than tragedy, involves chaotic natural conditions and a sense of inevitability as Christ submitted to the Father's will, and a violent, bloody death ("Tragedy and the Christian Faith," *Christianity and Literature* 22, no. 2 [Winter 1973] : 8-14).
10. Raphael, "Tragedy and Religion," *The Paradox of Tragedy,* pp. 37-68.
11. Cherbonnier, "Biblical Faith and the Idea of Tragedy," *The Tragic Vision and the Christian Faith,* ed. Nathan A. Scott, Jr., p. 26. Sylvan Barnet makes much the same point, citing A.C. Bradley as well as Hegel: "A.C. Bradley, who generally interpreted Shakespeare's tragedies without reference to Christianity, saw hints of regeneration in them and concluded, influenced probably by Hegel, that a tragedy suggests, among other ideas, that 'if we could see the whole, and the tragic facts in their true place in it, we should find them not abolished, of course, but so transmuted that they had ceased to be strictly tragic' [(*Shakespearean Tragedy* [London, 1950], p. 324)—Barnet's note]. Now, Christianity is dramatic, but it is not tragic, for . . . Christian teleology robs death of its sting" ("Some Limitations of a Christian Approach to Shakespeare," *ELH* 22 [June 1955], 85).
12. Cherbonnier, pp. 30-33.
13. Cherbonnier, pp. 16, 37. Much of this is Hegelian, especially the observation that the tragic hero chooses between two "goods" rather than between good and evil, and the shifting of tragic reconciliation from protagonist to spectator. See W.K. Wimsatt, Jr., and Cleanth Brooks, *Literary Criticism: A Short History,* p. 557.
14. Cherbonnier, p. 41.
15. Cherbonnier, p. 46.
16. Watkin, pp. 43, 49, 50. This extreme emphasis on the divine omniscience and omnipotence of Christ comes close to denying his real humanity, and is certainly at odds with the modern tendency to do full justice to his manhood: see E.J. Tinsley's comments about modern Christology, below. Watkin's attitude could be described also as a kind of "angelism," an attempt to escape the limitations of human insight.
17. Michel, "The Possibility of a Christian Tragedy," *Thought* 31 (Autumn 1956): 414-415.
18. Bryant, *Hippolyta's View,* pp. 113, 138.
19. Bryant, p. 150.

20. The allusion is to Bryant's "Shakespeare's Allegory: The Winter's Tale," *Sewanee Review* 63 (1955): 202-222, and occurs in Battenhouse's "Shakespearean Tragedy: A Christian Interpretation," *The Tragic Vision and the Christian Faith,* pp. 83-84.

21. Battenhouse, *Shakespearean Tragedy,* pp. 263, 25, 174.

22. Battenhouse, *Shakespearean Tragedy,* pp. 215, 222, 278.

23. Battenhouse, *Shakespearean Tragedy,* pp. 159, 162.

24. Battenhouse, *Shakespearean Tragedy,* pp. 192-197.

25. The label, affixed pejoratively by Roland M. Frye in *Shakespeare and Christian Doctrine,* p. 19, is nonetheless memorable. Frye lists, among others, S.L. Bethell, Nevil Coghill, Paul N. Siegel, Irving Ribner, and J.A. Bryant as members of this school, but implies that Knight's methodology is more or less typical.

26. Knight, *Shakespearean Production,* pp. 157-158.

27. Knight, *Shakespearean Production,* p. 157, and *The Wheel of Fire,* pp. 130, 209, 259, 262.

28. Glencross, "Christian Tragedy," *A Christian Approach to Western Literature,* ed. Aloysius A. Norton and Joan T. Nourse, pp. 67-68.

29. David E. Roberts, "Christian Faith and Greek Tragedy," *Religion in Life* 18 (1948): 83.

30. David Roberts, "Christian Faith and Greek Tragedy," p. 88.

31. Lynch, p. 79.

32. Lynch, pp. 70-73, 85-86.

33. Scott, *The Broken Center,* pp. 122, 123, 126, 129, 130, 131, 134-135. Scott refers to Fergusson's *The Idea of a Theatre* and to Krieger's *The Tragic Vision.*

34. Scott, *The Broken Center,* pp. 135, 137, 138.

35. Scott, *The Broken Center,* pp. 139, 141.

36. Tinsley, *Christian Theology and the Frontiers of Tragedy,* pp. 8-10.

37. Tinsley, *Christian Theology and Frontiers of Tragedy,* pp. 18-19.

38. Auden, "The Christian Tragic Hero," *The New York Times Book Review,* December 16, 1945, p. 1; and "Introduction," *The Portable Greek Reader,* pp. 21, 23.

39. Auden, *The Dyer's Hand,* p. 175. The moral reprobation of the tragic hero raises serious problems about how he can be made sympathetic. Shakespeare and Racine, Auden claims, tried to accomplish this by assigning him "noble poetry," though "both of them must have known in their heart of hearts that this was a conjuring trick." He concludes that "a completely satisfactory tragedy" is probably impossible in a Christian society (pp. 176-177).

40. Preston Roberts, "A Christian Theory of Dramatic Tragedy," *The New Orpheus,* pp. 256, 258.

41. Preston Roberts, pp. 268, 265.

42. Preston Roberts, pp. 278, 270, 284, 281.

43. Preston Roberts, pp. 272-273, 280.

44. Preston Roberts, pp. 278-279.

45. Cox, *Between Earth and Heaven,* pp. 7, 10.

46. Cox, pp. 33, 35, 47.

47. Henn, *The Harvest of Tragedy,* rev. ed., pp. 74, 76, 77.

48. Henn, pp. 268, 290-291, 78.

49. Niebuhr, "Humor and Faith," *Discerning the Signs of the Times,* pp. 111-131.

50. Kenneth Hamilton, "Comedy in a Theological Perspective," *Religion in Life* 41 (1972): 230-231.

51. Watkin, p. 41.
52. Forsyth, p. 90.
53. Forsyth, p. 93.
54. Auden, *The Dyer's Hand*, pp. 176-177.
55. Auerbach, *Mimesis*, p. 31.
56. Lynch, p. 95.
57. Quoted in Lynch, pp. 101-102, from Shaw's *An Essay on Going to Church* (Boston: John W. Luce, 1905), pp. 50-51.
58. Barry Ulanov, in *The Rhetoric of Christian Comedy*, makes the same point: "Writers of Christian comedy do not laugh to themselves. They share the laughter. But their weeping is silent, buried beneath great caterwauls of amusement. Fallen man, they keep telling us, is as much a comic as a tragic spectacle" (p. 78).
59. Lynch, p. 109.
60. Scott, *The Broken Center*, pp. 90, 105-106, 108.
61. Tinsley, *Christian Theology and the Frontiers of Tragedy*, pp. 23-24.
62. Scott, *Samuel Beckett*, pp. 102, 103.
63. Vos, *The Drama of Comedy*.
64. Vos rightly credits this three-part movement to Francis Fergusson's *The Idea of a Theater*.
65. Vos, *The Drama of Comedy*, p. 23.
66. Vos, *For God's Sake Laugh!*, pp. 37-38.
67. Vos, *For God's Sake Laugh!*, p. 38.
68. Vos, *The Drama of Comedy*, p. 26.
69. Vos, *For God's Sake Laugh!*, pp. 55-56.
70. Vos, *The Drama of Comedy*, pp. 24-25.
71. Vos, *For God's Sake Laugh!*, pp. 40-41, 45.
72. Cox, *The Feast of Fools*, pp. 140-141. Cf. the observation by Joseph C. McLelland that "Christ is God's Fool, the clown who calls in question every human pretension to be something—church as well as state. Human wisdom cannot take the questioning and lays violent hands on him. He is banished from the normal rule of law (*nomos*) because he has threatened its very being with his skeptical humor. His is a Passion demanding our passion. The drama is real and the stage marked off to include us all" (*The Clown and the Crocodile*, p. 102).

Chapter Six

1. Gunn, "Introduction: Literature and its Relation to Religion," *Literature and Religion*, pp. 27-28.
2. Fiedler, "Cross the Border, Close the Gap," *Playboy* (December 1969), pp. 230, 258.
3. Martin E. Marty and Dean G. Peerman, "Introduction: The Recovery of Transcendence," *New Theology No. 7*, ed. Martin E. Marty and Dean G. Peerman, p. 18.
4. Berger, "Theological Possibilities: Starting with Man," *A Rumor of Angels*.
5. Rahner, *Man at Play*, pp. 12, 18, 94-95, 8.
6. Rahner, pp. 69-70.
7. Cox, *The Feast of Fools*.
8. Miller, *Gods and Games*.
9. Neale, *In Praise of Play*, p. 197.
10. Dean, *Coming To*, p. 105.
11. Dean, p. 141.

LIST OF WORKS CITED

Altizer, T.J.J., and William Hamilton. *Radical Theology and the Death of God.* Indianapolis: Bobbs Merrill, 1966.

Arnold, Matthew. *Literature and Dogma.* New York: Macmillan, 1914.

———. "The Study of Poetry." In *Essays in Criticism, Second Series,* ed. S.R. Littlewood. New York: St. Martin's, 1964.

Auden, W.H. "The Christian Tragic Hero." *The New York Times Book Review,* December 16, 1945, pp. 1, 21.

———. *The Dyer's Hand and Other Essays.* New York: Random, 1962.

———. "Introduction" to *The Portable Greek Reader.* New York: Viking, 1950.

Auerbach, Erich. *Mimesis: The Representation of Reality in Western Literature,* trans. Willard R. Trask. Princeton, N.J.: Princeton Univ. Press, 1953.

Babbitt, Irving. "Humanism: An Essay at Definition." In *Humanism and America,* ed. Norman Foerster, New York: Farrar & Rinehart, 1930.

Barnet, Sylvan. "Some Limitations of a Christian Approach to Shakespeare." *ELH* 22 (June 1955): 81-92.

Barth, Karl. *The Epistle to the Romans,* trans. Edwyn C. Hoskyns. London: Oxford Univ. Press, 1933.

———. *The Humanity of God.* Richmond, Va.: John Knox, 1960.

Battenhouse, Roy W. "The Relation of Theology to Literary Criticism." *Journal of Bible and Religion* 13 (February 1945): 16-22.

———. "Shakespearean Tragedy: Its Art and Its Christian Premises." In *The Tragic Vision and the Christian Faith,* ed. Nathan A. Scott, Jr. New York: Association, 1957.

———. *Shakespearean Tragedy: Its Art and Its Christian Promises.* Bloomington: Indiana Univ. Press, 1969.

Bentley, Eric. *The Importance of Scrutiny.* New York: New York Univ. Press, 1964.

Berdyaev, Nicolas, *The Destiny of Man,* trans. Natalie Duddington. 2nd ed. London: Geoffrey Bles. 1945.

———. *Dream and Reality,* trans. Katherine Lampert. London: Geoffrey Bles, 1950.

———. *Freedom and the Spirit,* trans. Oliver F. Clarke. New York: Scribners, 1935.

———. *The Meaning of the Creative Act,* trans. Donald A. Lowrie. New York: Harper, 1955.

Berger, Peter. *A Rumor of Angels: Modern Society and the Rediscovery of the Supernatural.* Garden City, N.Y.: Doubleday, 1969.

Bethell, S.L. "Christianity and Culture: Replies to Mr. Lewis." *Theology* 40 (May 1940): 356-362.

———. *Essays on Literary Criticism and the English Tradition.* London: Denis Dobson, 1948.

———. *The Literary Outlook.* London: Sheldon, 1943.

Bradner, Leicester. *Incarnation in Religion and Literature.* Faculty Papers, 4th series. New York: Nat. Council of the Protestant Episcopal Church, 1957.

Brémond, Henri. *Prayer and Poetry,* trans. Algar Thorold. London: Burnes, Oates & Washbourn, 1927.

Brett, Ray. "The Function of Literary Imagery in Christian Understanding." *Christian Scholar* 36 (June 1953): 92-99.

Bridge, A.C. *Images of God: An Essay on the Life and Death of Symbols.* London: Hodder & Stoughton, 1960.

Brooks, Cleanth. "Christianity, Myth, and the Symbolism of Poetry." In *Christian Faith and the Contemporary Arts,* ed. Finley Eversole. New York: Abingdon, 1962.

———. *The Hidden God.* New Haven: Yale Univ. Press, 1963.

———. "Metaphor and the Function of Criticism." In *Spiritual Problems in Contemporary Literature,* ed. Stanley R. Hopper. New York: Harper, 1952.

———. *The Well Wrought Urn.* New York: Harcourt, Brace, 1947.

Bryant, J.A., Jr. *Hippolyta's View: Some Christian Aspects of Shakespeare's Plays.* Lexington: Univ. of Kentucky Press, 1961.

Buckley, Vincent. *Poetry and Morality.* London: Chatto & Windus, 1959.

Bultmann, Rudolph. "New Testament and Mythology." In *Kerygma and Myth,* ed. Hans Werner Bartsch, trans. Reginald H. Fuller. Rev. ed. New York: Harper, Harper Torchbooks, 1961.

Cairns, David. "Natural Theology." In *A Handbook of Christian Theology,* ed. Marvin Halverson and Arthur A. Cohen. New York: Meridian Books, 1958.

Cassirer, Ernst. *Language and Myth,* trans. Susanne Langer. New York: Harper, 1946.

Cherbonnier, Edmond LaB. "Biblical Faith and the Idea of Tragedy." In *The Tragic Vision and the Christian Faith,* ed. Nathan A. Scott, Jr. New York: Association, 1957.

Coleridge, Samuel Taylor. *Biographia Literaria,* ed. John Shawcross. 2 vols. London: Oxford Univ. Press, 1907.

List of Works Cited

Cox, Harvey. *The Feast of Fools: A Theological Essay on Festivity and Fantasy.* Cambridge, Mass.: Harvard Univ. Press, 1969.

Dean, William D. *Coming To: A Theology of Beauty.* Philadelphia: Westminster, 1971.

Eliot, T.S. *After Strange Gods: A Primer of Modern Heresy.* London: Faber & Faber, 1934.

———. *On Poetry and Poets.* New York: Farrar, Straus & Cudahy, 1957.

———. *Selected Essays.* 3rd ed. London: Faber & Faber, 1951.

———. *The Use of Poetry and the Use of Criticism.* London: Faber & Faber, 1933.

Elman, Paul. "Twice-Blessed Enamel Flowers: Reality in Contemporary Fiction." In *The Climate of Faith in Modern Literature,* ed. Nathan A. Scott, Jr. New York: Seabury, 1964.

Else, Gerald F. *Aristotle's Poetics: The Argument.* Cambridge, Mass.: Harvard Univ. Press, 1963.

Every, George. *Christian Discrimination.* London: Sheldon, 1940.

———. "In Defence of Criticism." *Theology* 41 (September 1940): 159-165.

———. "The Necessity of Scrutiny." *Theology* 38 (March 1939): 176-186.

———. *Poetry and Personal Responsibility.* London: S.C.M., 1949.

Farrer, Austin. *The Glass of Vision.* Westminster: Dacre, 1948.

———. *A Rebirth of Images.* Westminster: Dacre, 1949.

Fiedler, Leslie A. "Cross the Border, Close the Gap." *Playboy,* December 1969, pp. 151, 230, 252-254, 256-258.

Forsyth, P.T. *Christ on Parnassus: Lectures on Art, Ethic, and Theology.* London: Hodder & Stoughton, 1912.

Frye, Roland M. *Perspective on Man: Literature and the Christian Tradition.* Philadelphia: Westminster, 1961.

———. *Shakespeare and Christian Doctrine.* Princeton, N.J.: Princeton Univ. Press, 1963.

Gardiner, Harold C., ed. *Fifty Years of the American Novel, 1900-1950: A Christian Appraisal.* New York: Scribners, 1951.

———. *In All Conscience: Reflections on Books and Culture.* Garden City, N.Y.: Hanover, 1959.

———. *Norms for the Novel.* New York: America Press, 1953.

Glencross, A.F. "Christian Tragedy." In *A Christian Approach to Western Literature,* ed. Aloysius A. Norton and Joan T. Nourse. Westminster, Md.: Newman, 1961.

Gunn, Giles. "Literature and Its Relation to Religion." In *Literature and Religion,* ed. Giles Gunn. New York: Harper, 1971.

Hamilton, Kenneth. "Comedy in a Theological Perspective." *Religion in Life* 41 (Summer 1972): 222-232.

Hamilton, William. *The New Essence of Christianity.* New York: Association, 1966.

Hanna, Thomas L. "A Question: What Does One Mean by 'Religious Literature'?" In *Mansions of the Spirit,* ed. George A. Panichas. New York: Hawthorn Books, 1967.

Harmsel, Henrietta Ten. "Tragedy and the Christian Faith." *Christianity and Literature* 22, no. 2 (Winter 1973): 8-14.

Harned, David Baily. *Theology and the Arts.* Philadelphia: Westminster, 1966.

Hazelton, Roger. *New Accents in Contemporary Theology.* New York: Harper, 1960.

——. *A Theological Approach to Art.* New York: Abingdon, 1967.

Heines, Donald Scott. "Problems of Literary Criticism and Theological Perspectives." Unpublished dissertation. Columbia Univ., 1964.

Henn, T.R. *The Harvest of Tragedy.* Rev. ed. New York: Barnes & Noble, 1966.

Hepburn, Ronald W. "Poetry and Religious Belief." In *Metaphysical Beliefs,* ed. Alasdair MacIntyre. London: S.C.M., 1957.

Holthusen, Hans Egon. "What is Christian in a Christian Literature?" In *Christian Faith and the Contemporary Arts,* ed. Finley Eversole. New York: Abingdon, 1962.

Hulme, T.E. *Speculations,* ed. Herbert Read. 2nd ed. London: Routledge & Kegan Paul, 1936.

James, D.G. *Scepticism and Poetry: An Essay on the Poetic Imagination.* London: Allen & Unwin, 1937.

Jarrett-Kerr, Martin. *Studies in Literature and Belief.* London: Rockliff, 1954.

Jaspers, Karl. *Tragedy Is Not Enough,* trans. H.A.T. Reiche. London: Rockliff, 1954.

Jones, David. "Art and Sacrament." In *The New Orpheus: Essays Toward a Christian Poetic,* ed. Nathan A. Scott, Jr. New York: Sheed & Ward, 1964.

Keen, Sam. *Apology for Wonder.* New York: Harper, 1969.

——. *To a Dancing God.* New York: Harper, 1970.

Knight, G. Wilson. *The Christian Renaissance.* 2nd ed. New York: Norton, 1962.

——. *Shakespearean Production.* Evanston: Northwestern Univ. Press, 1964.

——. *The Wheel of Fire.* London: Oxford Univ. Press, 1930.

Krumm, John McGill. "Theology and Literature: The Terms of the Dialogue on the Modern Scene." In *The Climate of Faith in Modern Literature,* ed. Nathan A. Scott, Jr. New York: Seabury, 1964.

Langer, Susanne, *Philosophy in a New Key,* 3rd ed. Cambridge, Mass.: Harvard Univ. Press, 1957.

Leavis, F.R. *The Common Pursuit.* London: Chatto & Windus, 1952.

Leavis, Q.D. "Charlotte Yonge and 'Christian Discrimination.'" *Scrutiny* 12 (1943): 152-160.

Leeuw, Gerardus van der. *Sacred and Profane Beauty: The Holy in Art,* trans. David E. Green, preface by Mircea Eliade. New York: Holt, 1963.

Lewis, C.S. "Christianity and Culture." *Theology* 40 (March 1940): 166-179.

Lewis, H.D. *Morals and Revelation.* London: Allen & Unwin, 1951.

Luccock, Halford E. *Contemporary American Literature and Religion.* Chicago: Willett, Clark, 1934.

Lynch, William F. *Christ and Apollo: The Dimensions of the Literary Imagination.* New York: Sheed & Ward, 1960.

McCarron, Hugh. *Realization: A Philosophy of Poetry.* New York: Sheed & Ward, 1937.

Machen, Arthur. *Hieroglyphics.* New York: Knopf, 1923.

Mackintosh, Hugh Ross. *Types of Modern Theology: Schleiermacher to Barth.* New York: Scribners, 1937.

McLelland, Joseph C. *The Clown and the Crocodile.* Richmond, Va.: John Knox, 1970.

Macquarrie, John. *Twentieth-Century Religious Thought: The Frontiers of Philosophy and Theology, 1900-1960.* New York: Harper, 1963.

Maritain, Jacques. *Art and Scholasticism and The Frontiers of Poetry,* trans. Joseph W. Evans. New York: Scribners, 1962.

———. *Creative Intuition in Art and Poetry.* New York: Pantheon Books, 1953.

———. *The Degrees of Knowledge,* trans. Bernard Wall and Margot R. Adamson. London: Geoffrey Bles, 1937.

———. *The Responsibility of the Artist.* New York: Scribners, 1960.

———, and Raissa Maritain. *The Situation of Poetry,* trans. Marshall Suther. New York: Philosophical Library, 1955.

Marty, Martin E., and Dean G. Peerman. "Introduction: The Recovery of Transcendence." In *New Theology No. 7,* ed. Martin E. Marty and Dean G. Peerman. New York: Macmillan, 1970.

Mascall, Eric L. *Theology and Images.* London: Mowbray, 1963.

———. *Words and Images.* London: Longmans, Green, 1957.

Michel, Laurence. "The Possibility of a Christian Tragedy." *Thought* 31 (Autumn 1956): 403-428.

Miller, David L. *Gods and Games: Toward a Theology of Play.* New York: World, 1969.

Neale, Robert E. *In Praise of Play.* New York: Harper, 1969.

Nicholson, Norman. *Man and Literature.* London: S.C.M., 1943.

Niebuhr, Reinhold. *Beyond Tragedy: Essays on the Christian Interpretation of History.* New York: Scribners, 1937.

———. *Discerning the Signs of the Times.* New York: Scribners, 1946.

———. *An Interpretation of Christian Ethics.* New York: Harper, 1935.

———. *The Nature and Destiny of Man.* 2 vols. New York: Scribners, 1941.

Pottle, Frederick A. *Christian Teaching of Literature.* Faculty Papers, 3rd series. New York: Nat. Council of the Protestant Episcopal Church, 1956.

Rahner, Hugo. *Man at Play,* trans. B. Battershaw and E. Quinn. New York: Herder & Herder, 1967.

Ramsey, Arthur Michael. *An Era in Anglican Theology: From Gore to Temple.* New York: Scribners, 1960.

Randall, John H., Jr. *Aristotle.* New York: Columbia Univ. Press, 1960.

Raphael, David Daiches. *The Paradox of Tragedy.* London: Allen & Unwin, 1960.

130

Reist, John S., Jr. "Treading Water in the Acheron: A Study in the Nature and Function of Theological Literary Criticism." *Christian Scholar's Review* 2 (1972): 209-223.

Richards, I.A. *Principles of Literary Criticism.* New York: Harcourt, Brace, 1925.

Roberts, David E. "Christian Faith and Greek Tragedy." *Religion in Life* 18 (1948): 79-89.

———. *Existentialism and Religious Belief.* New York: Oxford Univ. Press, 1957.

Roberts, Michael. "The Moral Influence of Poetry." *Theology* 39 (January 1939): 16-25.

Roberts, Preston T., Jr. "A Christian Theory of Dramatic Tragedy." In *The New Orpheus: Essays Toward a Christian Poetic,* ed. Nathan A. Scott, Jr. New York: Sheed & Ward, 1964.

Root, H.E. "Beginning All Over Again." In *Soundings,* A.R. Vidler. Cambridge: Cambridge Univ. Press, 1962.

Ross, Malcolm. *Poetry and Dogma.* New Brunswick, N.J.: Rutgers Univ. Press, 1954.

Rougement, Denis de. "Religion and the Mission of the Artist." In *Spiritual Problems in Contemporary Literature,* ed. Stanley R. Hopper. New York: Harper, 1952.

Sayers, Dorothy L. *The Mind of the Maker.* New York: Harcourt, Brace, 1941.

Schwartz, Delmore. "The Vocation of the Poet in the Modern World." In *Spiritual Problems in Contemporary Literature,* ed. Stanley R. Hopper. New York: Harper, 1952.

Scott, Nathan A., Jr. *The Broken Center: Studies in the Theological Horizon of Modern Literature.* New Haven: Yale Univ. Press, 1966.

———. *Craters of the Spirit: Studies in the Modern Novel.* Washington: Corpus Books, 1968.

———. "Criticism and the Religious Frontier." In *Humanities, Religion, and the Arts Tomorrow,* ed. Howard Hunter. New York: Holt, 1972.

———. "Faith and Art in a World Awry." In *The Climate of Faith in Modern Literature,* ed. Nathan A. Scott, Jr. New York: Seabury, 1964.

———. "Maritain in His Role as Aesthetician." *The Review of Metaphysics* 8 (March 1955): 480-492.

———. *Modern Literature and the Religious Frontier.* New York: Harper, 1958.

———. *Negative Capability: Studies in the New Literature and the Religious Situation.* New Haven: Yale Univ. Press, 1969.

———. " 'New Heav'ns, New Earth': The Landscape of Contemporary Apocalypse." *Journal of Religion* 53 (1973): 1-35.

———. *Rehearsals of Discomposure: Alienation and Reconciliation in Modern Literature.* New York: Columbia Univ. Press, 1952.

———. "The Relation of Theology to Literary Criticism." *Journal of Religion* 33 (October 1953): 266-277.

———. "Religious Symbolism in Contemporary Literature." In *Religious Symbolism,* ed. F. Ernest Johnson. New York: Harper, 1955.

———. *Samuel Beckett.* New York: Hillary House, 1965.

——. "Theology and the Literary Imagination." In *Adversity and Grace: Studies in Recent American Literature*, ed. Nathan A. Scott, Jr. Chicago: Univ. of Chicago Press, 1968.

——. *The Wild Prayer of Longing: Poetry and the Sacred*. New Haven: Yale Univ. Press, 1971.

Scott-Craig, T.S.K. "Christianity and Poetry." *Theology* 41 (July 1940): 25-30.

Sewall, Richard. *The Vision of Tragedy*. New Haven: Yale Univ. Press, 1959.

Shaftesbury, Anthony [Ashley Cooper, Third] Earl of. *Characteristicks of Men, Manners, Opinions, Times*. 3 vols. 5th ed. Birmingham, England: John Baskerville, 1773.

Shelley, Percy Bysshe. *The Complete Works of Percy Bysshe Shelley*, ed. Roger Ingpen and Walter E. Peck. 10 vols. New York: Scribners, 1926-1930.

Spanos, William V. *The Christian Tradition in Modern British Verse Drama: The Poetics of Sacramental Time*. New Brunswick, N.J.: Rutgers Univ. Press, 1967.

Spingarn, J.E. *A History of Literary Criticism in the Renaissance*. 2nd ed. New York: Columbia Univ. Press, 1908.

Stallman, Robert Wooster. "The New Critics." In *Critiques and Essays in Criticism: 1920-1948*, ed. Robert Wooster Stallman. New York: Ronald, 1949.

Stewart, Randall. *American Literature and Christian Doctrine*. Baton Rouge: Louisiana State Univ. Press, 1958.

Strong, A.H. *The Great Poets and Their Theology*. Philadelphia: Griffith & Rowland Press, 1897.

Tate, Allen. *Essays of Four Decades:* Chicago: Swallow, 1968.

Temple, William. *Nature, Man and God*. London: Macmillan, 1940.

TeSelle, Sallie M. *Literature and the Christian Life*. New Haven: Yale Univ. Press, 1966.

Tillich, Paul. *The Interpretation of History*, trans. N.A. Rasetzski and Elsa L. Talmey. New York: Scribners, 1936.

——. "The Meaning and Justification of Religious Symbols." In *Religious Experience and Truth*, ed. Sidney Hook. New York: New York Univ. Press, 1961.

——. *The Protestant Era*, trans. James Luther Adams. Chicago: Univ. of Chicago Press, 1948.

——. *The Religious Situation*, trans. H. Richard Niebuhr. New York: Holt, 1932.

——. "The Religious Symbol." In *Religious Experience and Truth*, ed. Sidney Hook. New York: New York Univ. Press, 1961.

——. *Systematic Theology*. 3 vols. Chicago: Univ. of Chicago Press, 1951-1963.

——. *Theology of Culture*, ed. Robert Kimball, New York: Oxford Univ. Press, 1959.

Tinsley, E.J. *Christian Theology and the Frontiers of Tragedy*. Leeds, England: Leeds Univ. Press, 1963.

——. "The Incarnation and Art." In *The Church and the Arts*, ed. Frank J. Glendenning. London: S.C.M., 1960.

Turnell, Martin. *Poetry and Crisis.* London: Sands, 1938.

Ulanov, Barry. "The Rhetoric of Christian Comedy." In *The McAuley Lectures 1961: Literature as Christian Comedy.* W. Hartford, Conn.: St. Joseph College, 1962.

Vahanian, Gabriel. *The Death of God.* New York: Braziller, 1961.

——. *Wait Without Idols.* New York: Braziller, 1964.

Van Buren, Paul. *The Secular Meaning of the Gospel.* New York: Macmillan, 1963.

Vos, Nelvin. *The Drama of Comedy: Victim and Victor.* Richmond, Va.: John Knox, 1966.

——. *For God's Sake Laugh!* Richmond, Va.: John Knox, 1967.

Waggoner, Hyatt H. "William Faulkner's Passion Week of the Heart." In *The Tragic Vision and the Christian Faith,* ed. Nathan A. Scott, Jr. New York: Association, 1957.

Walker, Williston. *A History of the Christian Church.* New York: Scribners, 1918.

Watkin, E.I. *Poets and Mystics.* London: Sheed & Ward, 1953.

Wellek, René. *A History of Modern Criticism: 1750-1950.* 4 vols. New Haven: Yale Univ. Press, 1955-1965.

Wilder, Amos N. "Christianity and the Arts: The Historic Divorce and the Contemporary Situation." *Christian Scholar* 40 (December 1957): 261-168.

——. *Modern Poetry and the Christian Tradition.* New York: Scribners, 1952.

——. *The New Voice: Religion, Literature, and Hermeneutics.* New York: Herder & Herder, 1969.

——. "Poetry and Religion." In *Christian Faith and the Contemporary Arts,* ed. Finley Eversole. New York: Abingdon, 1962.

——. "Scholars, Theologians, and Ancient Rhetoric." *Journal of Biblical Literature* 75 (1956): 1-11.

——. *The Spiritual Aspects of the New Poetry.* New York: Harper, 1940.

——. *Theology and Modern Literature.* Cambridge, Mass.: Harvard Univ. Press, 1958.

Wimsatt, William K., Jr., and Cleanth Brooks. *Literary Criticism: A Short History.* New York: Knopf, 1959.

INDEX

This list includes literary critics, theologians, and philosophers, but not creative writers. Individuals who are both creative writers and critics are indexed only when they function as critics.

Index

Index